Financial Literacy for Tweens

Help Your Pre-Teen Develop Essential Knowledge in Making Wise Financial Decisions Over a Lifetime

K. Thomas

Please consult a licensed professional before attempting any techniques outlined in this book.

By reading this document, the reader agrees that under no circumstances is the author responsible for any losses, direct or indirect, that are incurred as a result of the use of the information contained within this document, including, but not limited to, errors, omissions, or inaccuracies.

Table of Contents

Introduction

Money, like emotions, is something you must control to keep your life on the right track. –Natasha Munson

Have you ever thought about what you could've done with all the money you've gotten for doing chores or helping a neighbor out? The answer will likely shock you.

How much would you have now if you saved half of the money you've ever gotten? Would you be able to buy something you could only dream of? Possibly. The only problem is, many of us want instant rewards which is why we choose to immediately spend the money we get from completing chores or doing extra work around the house.

Of course, you'd rather go to the movies with that money. At least you'll get to hang out with your friends, right? But what if you all decided to save half of your allowance for a year and at the end of the year you get to do something truly **extraordinary**? I'll bet you'll be happier putting some of your money aside for a bigger reward at the end of the **sacrifice**.

That is exactly what I want to help you understand and crave. You might think not spending your money as soon as you get it defeats the purpose of working for it, but when you go back to your savings and see what new options are available to you, it'll be worth it.

My goal is to give you the knowledge you need to make smart financial choices and reap its sweet rewards because it's never too early to be empowered. Join me on this journey as I share the ins and outs of saving, investing, budgeting, and avoiding debt. Who wouldn't want to learn how to make their money last and stretch as far as possible, as well as save up for much bigger things?

You could leave the house right now and see something you'd absolutely love to have but because you know your parents can't afford it or won't get it for you, you accept it as being too much. Nothing is too much and you can achieve anything you want. All it costs is knowledge, discipline, and hard work.

Thankfully, I can give you all the knowledge you need about being money smart and the rest is up to you.

Learning how to spend your money wisely now will save you from making poor financial choices when you're older and help you avoid falling into the financial traps most adults fall into. You might be thinking you're not even close to having to worry about how to spend your money or on what, but why wait until then?

Taking the first steps to educate yourself now will only mean you'll get better over time. And by the time you actually do have to think about it, you'll not only have already built the foundation for a stable financial future, but you'll also be able to grow from there and surpass your expectations.

Your future is yours and yours alone.

Continue reading for in-depth insight into what it takes to develop good financial habits so that you can take control of your financial stability and **independence**, and avoid the most common financial pitfalls!

Chapter 1:
Understanding Money

A penny saved is a penny earned. –Benjamin Franklin

We all know money is an agreed-upon item of trade and **exchange** in the economy. It is used to trade a range of things like clothing, food, property, and more. Of course, the value of it depends on each specific country, but the basic concept of it remains. Everyone knows what it is, the value it holds, and understands that we need it when we buy something we'd like to buy or a service we want to use.

Introducing money basically got rid of the need for people to have something to exchange in order to get something else, as people can now simply pay for the item they want. Meaning past methods of trade, like trading one item for another (also known as barter), is not necessary anymore. As amazing as this is, there have been times in the past when money lost its value, which led people to bring back earlier trading methods.

With that, we can say with some level of certainty that many people didn't and still don't properly understand how the value of money changes. This might be why they struggle to plan ahead or ignore the importance of it.

Investing and securing your financial future is also not as common as it should be, and this can cause major problems in the long term.

Take the world's economic position after World War II, for example. Because of the price controls the French, British, and American armies placed on Germany, money had little to no value. People no longer wanted to exchange their material goods for a **currency** that was losing its value at such a fast pace. This led them to bring back trade through barter. It took major changes years later to allow an economy of money to replace the barter economy (Fontinelle, n.d.).

Use Money as a Store of Value, Medium of Exchange, and a Unit of Account

Store of value means storing or **preserving** the value of something. Since the value of goods can't exactly be stored, money can be used to store value. This is done by investing or saving it for use at a later stage. What the invested money is worth depends on whether it gains interest over time or how strong that specific currency is when you choose to make use of it again. Some goods like silver or gold can also be used as stores of value;

however, money is the most commonly used commodity.

The **medium of exchange** involves the basic purpose of money. Exchanging money to carry out a purchase of goods and services. And while we have seen goods being exchanged for goods, money is more acceptable as the way of payment because of its potential to rise in value and how widely accepted it is as the primary purchase method.

The **unit of account** involves something being able to be exchanged, identified, and calculated. If you're still sure what I mean by this, think of it this way: The item or service can be identified by all, exchanged for a particular item, and the value can be calculated easily.

These are all the traits that have given money its position in economic trade and are the reason people are eager to gain as much of it as possible.

The Role of Government and Central Banks

These institutions are in control of printing, regulating, and controlling the supply of money. But why?

Well, all major countries use monetary systems which usually consist of three levels.

They are:

- **Holders**—Also known as the public. The holders are not only regular people but also include smaller businesses.

- **Commercial banks**—They are companies offering financial services to businesses, individuals, and governmental corporations.

- **Central banks**—They are the national organizations that control matters relating to certain kinds of money. They also offer financial services to their country's government, as well as commercial banks.

The Different Forms of Money

Money can actually be just about anything as long as everyone has agreed to it and accept the chosen item as having monetary value. This means whatever thing people choose to be money can be used to trade one thing for another.

You might be surprised to learn that tobacco, cigarettes, beads, livestock, and copper are some of the goods that were used in older days as a form of money. Of course, money has since been upgraded and adjusted to suit the needs of the people of its time period. Can you imagine going into a store today and offering the shopkeeper a chicken or a bag of beads for a pack of sodas and a snickers bar? Surely not, the shopkeeper will think it's some kind of prank.

Anyway, let's discuss some of the different types of money found today.

- **Fiat money**—This is coins and paper money whose value is set by the governments of a country. Its value either increases or decreases depending on the economic market's supply and demand. This kind of money is heavily controlled to avoid poor management of it, which can be harmful to a country's economy.

- **Commercial bank money**—This kind of money involves financial accounts people have with the commercial banks who store their money. The money here is paid into the account through online or electronic transfers, cash deposits, or cheques and can be withdrawn from an ATM, in-person in the bank, through online banking or bank drafts, or through cheques. **Withdrawing** your money this way means you get it immediately and you don't have to give any form of notice to the bank.

- **Fiduciary money**—Here we are talking about money approved by governments, where the money is constantly being passed through the economy. It is more often paid in paper money; however, silver and gold, banknotes, cheques, and digital money like Bitcoin, is also accepted as fiduciary money—as long as it has the same value. These sales are based on trust between those involved, as well as the trust in the value of that money.

- **Commodity money**—This kind of money is used to exchange goods and services. The value of it depends on the value of the resource being used and is decided by those involved in the exchange systems. Native metals like copper, silver, and gold are used as commodity money; however, commodity money has improved over the years. The value still depends on the availability of the resource, for example, pearls, tea, shells, gold coins, sugar, iron, and more have all been used as commodity money at some point but some of them have no monetary value anymore and some of them still do.

These are only some of the most popularly used types of money; however, there are many other forms as well.

Such as

- **Credit cards**—This is not money but a token of money. A person who needs money will go to a bank or financial institute who will then do checks on that person's ability to repay the money they want to borrow. That institute will then load the credit card with digital money. The borrowed money is repaid monthly, and the amount depends on how much credit the borrower was given and the interest rates on those funds. This is known as *debt*.

- **Debit cards**: This involves opening an account at a bank; however, the money you can withdraw is not borrowed to you. Instead, that is the money you get through payments from your employer or whoever is transferring it into your account. This money can be withdrawn immediately with no **assessment** on repayment habits because the bank takes their fees immediately with each transaction.

- **Crypto currency**: This is a form of digital money or tokens, and is not controlled by the government or central banks. Their value depends on what people are willing to pay for it and these payments are done through online programs. While there are many different cryptocurrencies out there, people are most familiar with Ether and Bitcoin.

When we speak about wealth, the immediate thought that comes to mind is lots of money and belongings, but wealth is so much more than that.

A person can have lots of money but if they have tons of debt (because they live an expensive lifestyle or whatever) their money goes as quickly as it comes, and it often leaves them with little-to-nothing.

You wouldn't consider this wealthy, would you?

Of course, not. The best way to view wealth is having enough money to last you a long time rather than a lot of money that will be finished in a short time.

An easy way to check if someone is wealthy, is to pretend they can't work for a while, for whatever reason, and won't have a monthly income coming in for that time. People who are not wealthy will have to make a plan as soon as possible, because they won't be able to support themselves or their families without that money.

Whereas someone who is wealthy won't have to run around trying to make a plan, because they can go for a long time without their monthly income. These are people who are getting money from places other than their job alone and they can take care of themselves and their family for months and sometimes years, without the income from the job they have lost.

They can do more than just take care of themselves; they can still live the life they were living when they were receiving a monthly income, meaning they don't have to move to a smaller house, eat cheap food, cut out certain activities just to survive.

The money they get from places that aren't their jobs is called passive income, and it is what separates the wealthy from those that merely have lots of money.

This is what it means to be wealthy.

Money; however, is obviously the commodity today needed to become wealthy. If your job pays you a lot of money but you can't survive without that monthly income, you are still not wealthy. You just get a lot of money monthly. Even if your expenses are not too high but you have no way of surviving long enough without the money from that job, you are still not wealthy.

Understanding the Value of Money and How It Changes Over Time

The time value of money (TVM), also called the present

discounted value or net present value (NPV), is basically the idea that money is more valuable at the present time than at a later stage. The reason for this idea is that money you have now can be put into investments which would lead to that money earning returns over time (growing in value), rather than using that same amount of money in the future.

How does the money grow in value, you ask? It earns interest.

This is only possible if you put that money into savings accounts because they have a certain percentage of interest the money will increase in value, either monthly or annually.

Keeping the money aside without putting it into such accounts means the value of that money goes down faster than you can say, "Show me the money."

The money won't necessarily be less valuable when you want to use it, but if you know you don't plan to use that money and don't invest it, you will definitely lose out on all the additional money you could've earned on top of that **initial** amount.

Inflation: What It Is and How It Affects Purchasing Power

Inflation refers to the rise in prices of our daily goods and services. So naturally, when the price of something goes up it causes the value of your money to go down.

This means after inflation, you can buy less goods with the same amount of money compared to what you could've bought in the past. Therefore, inflation has a negative impact on the TVM. No matter how small the rise in prices is, your purchase power is affected.

It's important to think about how inflation and purchasing power will affect the returns of your investment, because that amount will be taken from your overall total when you collect your returns. Interest rates and how the economy in your country is growing also plays a big role in how valuable your money is right now and will be in the future.

The longer you leave your money in a savings account, the more interest that money builds. That means your money is making more money just by staying put in that account. If the currency in your country is always growing, then you stand a good chance of having a great return even after the effects of inflation.

Saving and investing your money is a sure way to grow your wealth and not rely on the money you get each week or each month from your allowance. It can't be fun using up all your money and having nothing until the next time someone gives you money again.

Understanding TVM is important when making investment decisions because you'll be able to see how much money you will get out of it and how long it will take to get there. So, you should learn how to track the TVM to help you make smart investment decisions.

The Importance of Money Management and Financial Literacy

You might wonder what financial literacy is, and it is quite straightforward.

It's nothing but a better way of saying knowing how to work wisely with your money. This doesn't only mean investing, saving, and budgeting. It also means you know how to manage your money in such a way that you can use it and also make it grow.

Financial literacy is extremely important because it will stop you from wasting or spending your money carelessly. There is no time like the present to set yourself up for a positive financial journey and learn better and simpler ways to manage your money as you grow older.

Why Should I Become Financially Literate?

Not knowing how to best work with your money puts you at risk of picking up bad spending habits, mountains of debt, falling victim to scams, and failing to have good long-term plans for your future.

These are only some negatives that come with financial illiteracy.

Every person who works and earns money should be able to secure a good retirement. If they can't, there might be something they are doing wrong and not even know it. Most young adults today have fallen into the trap of payday loans, **pawnshops**, and turning to finance services just to make it until their next paycheck.

Here are some ways financial literacy will benefit you:

- **Empowerment**: It will empower you to make your own choices about how to spend your money, and you can trust they are properly informed decisions.

- **Staying one step ahead**: This means you will be able to stay a step ahead of emergencies, so even if something unexpected happens, you won't have to break yourself to fix it. Considering how uncertain the value of money is, it is better to be prepared for anything.

- **Achieve your goals**: This knowledge helps you understand how to save and plan your budget which is very useful when you have a specific goal you want to achieve. If there's something you hope to buy but can't afford immediately, your financial knowledge allows you to create a plan of how to get there.

- **Self-assurance and independence**: Many people make poor decisions when faced with a financial crisis, but financial literacy gives you the self-assurance to make serious life choices with no regrets or doubts. This level of self-assurance also comes with great independence. Even if one or two of the choices you make don't always go according to plan, you won't be overcome with fear about future decisions. You will accept it as a learning curve.

- **Prevent lasting damage**: Making use of financial services may seem like a good idea in the present but once you are financially literate, you will be able to weigh your options and consider the lasting effects of your choices more clearly. This will help prevent causing lasting damage to your financial growth.

As you can see, financial literacy isn't only about understanding how the value of money increases or decreases over time, it is also about proper management of that money in the present and future so that you can get the most out of your money and not just survive.

There are five primary elements that make up financial literacy.

These are:

- **Taxation or tax**—Knowing the many types of taxes and how the rates affect your **inheritance**, income, and investments offers you a better chance at financial stability.

- **Investments**—Investing involves more than simply putting your money away into savings, stocks or assets. You can **maximize** your income if you **prioritize** understanding how price levels, risk reduction, interest rates, indexes, and expansion works.

- **Borrowing**—Borrowing money from finance companies is often **unavoidable**, but with financial literacy you learn to do so without causing more harm to your finances. This means you will need to understand how compound interest, payment periods, interest rates, loan structure, and time value of money affects your income and investments.

- **Budgets**: A good budget allows you to pay off any debt you have while still having money for you to save and spend. Balance is the key when creating your budget as you will be able to **distribute** your money everywhere you'd like it to go and still secure your financial growth and security. Your budget should be a layout of how much of your money you will save, spend, invest, and possibly donate.

- **Managing your personal finances**: This is basically just the mixture of all the above elements. It helps you lower your debt and how much money you need to borrow by increasing your savings and investments.

  Effective management of your personal finances include

  - setting up a budget that tracks (whether on an app or by journal) how much money you get monthly, your total monthly expenses (money you have no choice but to spend), total luxury items (going out with friends or treats), and savings.

  - placing your savings goals above all else. Meaning you need to figure out exactly how much money to put away towards a long-term goal and stick to it monthly.

○ paying off any debt you have first. It may come with sacrifice but when you no longer have to pay this amount monthly you will surely feel the relief.

○ keeping tabs on your credit score and report. This is the yearly report financial service providers upload information about your repayment habits onto. It displays how much debt you owe, who you owe it to, and how well you are paying it back.

○ securing your retirement. Put money away for when you are older and can't work anymore. You never know what the future holds or how long you will be able to work, so having a retirement plan saves you from having to rely on money you earn in the future. The money you put away in your youth will be a great help in your old age.

○ paying your bills on time. This is another way to ensure you have good borrowing habits. Paying your bills as soon as they are due will look good on your credit report and will open doors for more **constructive** borrowing. Just be sure not to overdo it and make sure the bills are paid in full and on time. Either set up reminders on your phone or make use of automatic debits.

Setting Financial Goals

Setting goals in life is a great way to keep you motivated and working hard. You know what you want, why you want it, when you want, so you will do whatever it takes to get there.

Financial goals are no different. They are not the same as financial planning or budgeting though, even though it may seem that way.

Financial goals are milestones you want to reach at a certain point in your life. Let's say you want to save $50,000 in five years. That is not a financial plan or budget, but rather a financial goal. Of course, it will be easier to turn into a reality with the help of financial planning and budgeting, but in the end it's a goal. The goal doesn't have to be such a large amount or for such a long period, but I'm sure you get the gist of it.

Your goals should be in line with the amount of money you expect to receive monthly, your personal hopes, and principles.

Different Types of Financial Goals

As I said previously, all your goals don't have to be for long periods or large amounts of money. There can be smaller goals you'd like to **accomplish** as you work your way toward your bigger goals.

Giving your goals specific names, like "first car" or "vacation in Cabo", for example, helps you to **visualize** your goal and makes it that much more important.

We can divide financial goals into three types.

- **Short-term**—These goals extend as far as three years only and can either be set out to help you achieve something you'd like in the near future, or it can bring you closer to goals in the far future.

- **Mid-term**—Mid-term goals are pretty long, but can range anywhere between three to ten years and are usually not related to quick pleasures like vacation trips. It could be anything from paying off all your debt to saving enough money to start a small business.

- **Long-term**—They are goals that take a lot of time and effort and are harder to stay motivated for, since the rewards are so far away. They usually take over ten years to achieve but offer the biggest rewards. Long-term goals consist of smaller goals and often achieving the short or mid-term goals make it easier to achieve the long-term ones. For example, buying a house or apartment of your own, putting a large amount toward your retirement, or expanding your business.

The idea of setting these goals is to allow yourself a realistic amount of time to reach each **milestone** and having a sure reward at the end of each of it. Eventually, you might even want to speak to a financial advisor to help you better strategize how to **monopolize** your funds and get more than you are already getting out of your money. Passive incomes are a terrific way to do this, but you need to be sure that you know what you are doing, or **enlist** the assistance of someone who can guide you effectively.

It's also important to remember that life doesn't always go exactly according to plan, so if you hit a few bumps along the way, don't stress. It happens to the best of us. Still, it's better to be consistent and keep going than to quit and wander **aimlessly** into the future with no idea of how you are going to make it.

Chapter 2:
Budgeting Basics

Don't tell me what you value, show me your budget, and I'll tell you what you value. –Joe Biden

Budgeting isn't only for people with low income. It's highly **advisable** that all people create a budget. It helps you follow a strict spending program and ensures that you prioritize your money properly. Your financial future depends on you making smart choices in your youth so you don't end up in a bad situation as you draw closer to retirement.

It also makes achieving your goals a lot easier than if you spend your money left, right, and center, without having a **strategy**.

How It Produces Effective Financial Planning

The main way that budgeting results in effective financial planning is through highlighting poor spending habits. Many of us don't look close enough at our spending trends to see how many things we buy without actually needing them.

Sure, we have reasons why we buy the things we do, but are those reasons really good enough?

For instance, if you're paying the highest price for hundreds of channels and reason that it's for the children or sports channels that you can't get anywhere else, or because regular cable plans are too **limited** to enjoy, are you being truly honest with yourself?

Who actually watches every single channel or even half of the channels available on extended cable plans? This is only an example of **unnecessary** expenses we tell ourselves we need.

By budgeting, it forces you to look closer at how and why you spend your money. It also forces you to cut out expenses you don't really need as well as gain a **vital** sense of self-control, even when you have more than enough money to buy whatever it is.

Aside from curbing overspending, budgeting also helps reduce the amount of financial strain or stress on your shoulders. Even though it's not much fun having to sit and calculate where every penny should go, another reward for this boring task is that your finances won't overwhelm you.

You would be readily prepared for the unexpected and surely rise above the temptations many people struggle with.

Furthermore, it also allows you to stay ahead of any potential setbacks and safeguards you from some of the **devastating** effects these setbacks can have. Additionally, you gain new **insight** on what income is and how your spending impacts how much income you have. The great thing about this part of financial planning is you'll become so good at predicting how your money flows in and out, that you'll know which months will need you to be more careful and which months offer you a bit more freedom.

This is always a great thing to do because everyone has financial highs and lows, so being able to sort of foresee when you'll have those lows pressures you to be smarter during your highs, as it'll help keep you balanced and get you through the tougher times.

This strategy is essential when you have big dreams and goals like buying a fancy new car, house, or even if you just want to join your friends on an exotic vacation. You'll know beforehand that those aren't things you can afford to do in the heat of the moment, which means planning and budgeting is your most powerful tool to achieve this.

Because effective financial planning reduces anxiety caused by financial stress, you can rest easy knowing that your life is on track. I can't tell you how many adults with good-paying jobs still have sleepless nights because they can't cope with their list of expenses and debt.

The reality is, they earn enough to take good care of themselves but because of **reckless** spending habits and having no proper plan for how to make up for those losses or change such behavior, they're constantly stressed out and waiting on that next paycheck to get them through.

This could all be avoided if they only took the time to examine how much money they make, how much they have to spend, and how much they can save.

Finally, budgeting allows you to remain organized as you pay your bills on time and as such, avoid penalties, late fees, and **accumulating** tons of debt.

The Process of Creating a Budget and Sorting Spending Priorities

Now, as ideal as it is to start budgeting, many of us struggle to even get started. Mainly because we don't know exactly what the budget should include and exclude, or where to even begin.

Let's go through the step-by-step process of creating your budget and how to prioritize the most important expenses first.

Track Income and Expenses to Establish a Starting Budget

In order to establish how to start your budget, there are some essential points that can't be missed.

- Figure out what your net income is. This is what you receive in your bank account from your employer and it forms the basis of a good budget. We'll discuss why you shouldn't use your total income as the basis for your budget in more detail later on.

  For people who don't receive a set amount of money each month (get paid for each job they do, for example, someone who is self-employed or a freelancer), it's best to keep all records of income in order to work out an **estimated average** you can expect monthly.

- Monitor spending habits. This step follows after you know how much money you are getting in. You can now see where all that money is going. Make a list of everything you buy each month so you can see what you're spending the most on. This is a key part of seeing where unnecessary expenses come in.

- Start planning. Now that you know how your money is coming and going, you can determine what kind of plan you need. Start by prioritizing the most important things in your life like food, housing, transport and insurance. Have a look at how much all these are costing you and be honest with yourself about whether the amount is acceptable or if you'd like to spend less.

  It might be helpful to set a cap for each expense to prevent you from going over what you are willing to spend on those. This will give you a clear idea of how much your non-negotiable necessities will amount to in the months to come.

Identify Areas You Can Cut Costs

Next, look closer at the money you spend on things you can do without. This might be social events with friends, new clothes each month, online subscriptions, takeouts etc. **Sieve** through these expenses and see what you can use less of and what can be cut-out entirely for a few months.

Looking at the list of things you're buying monthly, you may think you're already not spending a lot of money so why should you cut costs?

Well, this is where the next part of the process comes in.

- Set achievable goals. It might be hard to want to cut costs when you don't realize or haven't given much thought to some **significant** things you want in life. Remodeling your room, having an entire wardrobe makeover, or going somewhere special, may be some of the things you don't even know are on the list of things you want.

  Once you actually take the time to think about things you'd like, it becomes easier to set these goals and do what's needed to make it happen.

- Make changes to spending habits so you can stay on budget. Having a clear idea of your income, expenses, and goals gives you the motivation you need to start shifting funds around and cutting some expenses entirely. The place that should be the easiest to remove costs and make reductions is usually in the **category** of things you want.

Takeouts every single weekend is not a necessity, so this is a good example of where you can make adjustments. Another could be having overly expensive or multiple **colognes**. There's nothing wrong with wanting to smell good, but it shouldn't be at the cost of an even greater reward.

Be sure to separate these additional expenses into categories under needs and wants. Also, don't fool yourself into thinking something is a need just because you can't imagine life without it. Further, don't expect to see major changes from the get-go. The first step is to let go of some of the things you don't really need but have gotten used to.

Once you've seen the change in your savings, it'll motivate you to make slightly bigger changes. For instance, you might realize that driving to the store down the road is a waste when it's just for bread and milk, so you'll take a walk there and save the gas for when you really need it.

Trust the process and know that these minor changes will soon make a big difference.

Update and Review Regularly

No one is perfect and sometimes we spend more than we mean to without even noticing. Don't worry, this is not the end of the world. However, this is exactly why we review the budget often.

The review shows us whether we are doing what we're supposed to and getting where we want to be. Tracking your spending isn't the only reason to review your budget. You might have received an increase or drop on your income or added a necessary expense, all of which call for a budget update.

If you don't do this, your budget isn't a true representation of your financial situation and this can create new problems.

Understanding Income, Expenses, and Savings

Okay, I know you've taken in a lot with the setting up of a budget, but now it's time to learn what income, expenses, and savings really mean.

Most people have the basic idea of what counts as what; however, to prevent any issues during the setting up of your budget, I'd like to offer a proper description of each.

Income

As you know, this is the money you get (by earning or being given) in a particular period. It could be daily, weekly, monthly, or yearly. For people working for their income, the term wages or salary is most appropriate.

Other incomes, possibly coming from earning interest, deposit accounts, or investments are seen plainly as income.

Expenses

This refers to the services and goods we use as we carry out our daily duties. It's important to note that expenses are recurring, which means it's what we pay continuously, for example, your home (rent or mortgage), water, gas, and electricity bills, food and more.

Savings

Savings doesn't have to mean only retirement funds. People put money into savings for many things, particularly things that cost a large amount of money that typically can't be paid all at once.

For instance, a lot of people save for their child's tertiary education, new cars, new homes, family vacations, but most importantly: Unexpected events. Living from paycheck-to-paycheck doesn't seem so bad when nothing unexpected happens; until it does. Anything that requires money when you aren't prepared for it, can cause you to go into panic.

An unplanned pregnancy, a health complication, or a car accident all require immediate funds and these are the kind of unexpected events that can leave people **bankrupt**. Savings offer you the freedom to face situations like these with a clear head because, even though unplanned, the financial part of it is sorted.

Understanding the Difference Between Gross and Net Income

At some point, if not already, you're bound to come across these terms. It's vital that you know what their differences are though, because not knowing can land you in some pretty undesirable situations.

- **Gross income**—Usually calculated as the amount of money you earn in a year but also used as a calculation of money earned monthly. This money; however, is the money earned before any **deductions** have been made. The deductions made on this amount are usually to cover taxes, company insurance (if you have), or development and training (if you work for a company that does this regularly). This total amount appears on your salary slip but is not paid to you.

- **Net income**—This is what gets paid into your bank account and if you have an employer, you'll notice it as the second largest sum on your salary slip. It's the amount you get after all the **mandatory** deductions have already been made and is the number you can work with as your actual monthly income.

Identifying Sources of Income

While income can be given as a gift or allowance, it's primarily earned either through selling labor or capital.

When you sell labor, it just means you work for your money and when you sell capital, it just means you invest.

Selling capital is nothing more than taking money and using it to make more money. An example of this would be lending money to people in need of it and charging interest. The interest you charge is, in essence, your income in that respect.

Investing doesn't only have to be in property or stocks, it can also be done through collecting coins, **antiques**, livestock, or art. The idea is to put money into something that can return more money later on. Of course, as long as the item you invest in can be resold and bring you money later it's an investment, but who would want to invest in something that won't generate more money than they initially put in?

Understanding the Different Types of Expenses

As explained earlier, expenses are costs that are so regular that you have no choice but to make monthly provision for it. These bills include education fees, gas, food, car payments, etc.

The **recurring** expenses are harder to make adjustments to but you might be able to cut back on some of them. You will also find that unforeseen expenses can creep up on you. They're often things like fixing a leaking pipe in your home or having your car checked and so on.

If you need help checking exactly what your monthly expenses are, you can go through your bank statements and highlight them as they appear. Try color-coding it to make it easier to see what can be classed as recurring and what is unexpected.

If you don't spend via card, so in cash, it's time to start **journaling** what you spend daily, either on paper or on an app on your phone. That way you can separate your expenses and list them accordingly.

Setting a Portion of Your Income Aside for Savings

Savings, as you've seen, is for a wide range of things. Of course, one of the best things to save for is your retirement because no matter how fit you are now, we all reach an age when we can no longer work the way we used to.

This is one of the most important and common savings types. That said, people have also realized that there's no way to control what happens. Even if you have a foolproof plan in place and strictly stick to it, anything can happen.

For this reason, savings has been introduced as a way to give people peace of mind in unforeseen circumstances. Other savings are for things we want to buy but don't want to or can't bear the burden of giving out large sums of money in one spending. The key to effective savings is not only to put the money aside and avoid using those funds when calculating your **affordability**, but to put it as far as possible from the money you plan to spend. It's simpler this way, as the urge to spend it is eliminated by doing so.

You don't have to choose savings accounts, but people usually go for this option because of the interest they'll gain on their money. That acts as greater motivation to leave the funds where it is so you don't disrupt the interest you'll receive on it.

It's common for people to have the desire to save, but due to the lack of understanding of the best saving strategies, they fail miserably and give up.

When people think of how to organize or arrange savings, they often think that this is done by taking their income, deducting their expenses, and whatever's left can be placed into savings. However, this is a critical mistake.

Obviously, your expenses are extremely important and need to be paid, but if you give it more priority over savings, you'll end up creating excuses for why you can't save or why you don't have a set amount going into your savings. There's absolutely nothing wrong with treating yourself to something nice from time-to-time, but many times we give in to the urge to buy ourselves something every single month and this is where the problem comes in.

When you arrange your savings by taking your income, deducting your savings, and leaving whatever's left for your expenses, you stand a better chance of spending only what you need to. This is because the only money that's left is the money that has to go to certain places and you can't convince yourself that spending it won't do much harm, since you know it will.

Needless to say, doing this is going to be hard. It'll take an enormous amount of discipline every single month but I promise, it will be worth it. If you do want to buy yourself something nice on occasion, you can always prepare for it ahead of time and save slightly extra in the months before you make the purchase.

That means your savings aren't taking a hit because of that item.

Many people who started saving late in life regret not starting as soon as they earned their first paycheck and some even feel they would've been able to see a bigger difference in their life had they started with their allowance. Saving isn't only about the pleasure of having money to turn to when you have nothing coming in.

This habit also offers extreme discipline, financial intelligence, and security that most of society lacks. That is why people stress over losing their jobs or worldwide **pandemics**, because they have nothing to fall back on.

Deciding How Much Should Go to Savings

There is a rule in finance referred to as the 50/30/20 budget rule, and it is rapidly increasing in popularity (Whiteside, n.d. para.1).

What the rule suggests is that 50% of your net income has to be used to pay all your non-negotiable expenses (expenses that can't go unpaid), 30% of it can go to unfixed expenses, and 20% should be placed into savings.

This seems highly doable, right?

I mean, you're getting 30% of your net income to spend on things you don't exactly need, so what more do you want?

But remember, just because 30% of it can be used for things you want doesn't mean you have to spend the full amount or any of it every single month. There may be months that you just feel like eating out once or buying something small, and then there'll be months when you'll feel like being a little more **extravagant** with your self-care and rewards. What you can do to have a healthy balance of that 30%, is to use only what you really want and whatever you have left of it can be placed into a separate savings.

That savings would then be purely for your wants and you can withdraw money from it whenever you want without it affecting your primary savings.

The 20% for savings doesn't all have to go to one account either. A portion of it can be used to build interest and another portion can be used as your emergency fund. The idea is to distribute your money in a smart and rewarding fashion, while still prioritizing your future and unexpected situations.

How to Identify Fixed and Flexible Expenses

What Is a Fixed Expense?

Fixed expenses are expenses that are a constant must. Even if you change the amounts by choosing something cheaper, that expense is still there. It may be less now, but it is there either way—like your rent, for example. Even if you move to a cheaper place, your rent is still a fixed expense because it's still there, only now it's lower than what you paid before.

Something to remember when it comes to fixed expenses is even though it occurs regularly, the frequency of it doesn't also have to be monthly. It could be weekly, **fortnightly**, **quarterly**, or **annually**.

Also, the amounts may not always be the same amount.

Say a cellphone bill, for instance, they might charge you around the same amount but the exact amount differs with each bill. It could be because of making more calls that month or spending more time on the internet. However, even though there are slight changes in the amounts, you usually have a rough idea how much they will charge you before the bill arrives.

Examples of some fixed expenses are

- education fees
- car payments
- insurance
- cellphone
- internet
- loans
- gym subscriptions
- mortgage or rent

Fixed expenses are your friend when setting up your budget, because they allow you the ability to better plan how your money can be **assigned**. This obviously makes it easier when sticking to the 50/30/20 budget rule.

What Is a Flexible Expense?

Flexible expenses, sometimes also called variable expenses, are expenses that regularly change and are likely linked to your actions and choices. These expenses don't come as often as fixed expenses and the amounts are not as predictable.

It doesn't always mean that flexible expenses are ones you don't need or don't have to pay, it simply means that they are not as constant as fixed expenses.

Because of this, there is a level of uncertainty when it comes to these bills. Fuel or medical bills fall into this category because the amounts between periods often differ hugely. One month you might drive more than the previous one, so it goes without saying the amount will be higher.

It's common for people to have a hard time tracking and making proper **provision** for flexible expenses, because of how hard it is to predict how much it would cost them.

This isn't the case with all flexible expenses as some can be controlled to a certain extent, like daily and monthly groceries.

Examples of some flexible expenses are

- home and car maintenance (repairs and upkeep)
- personal care
- fuel
- groceries
- clothes

- medical fees

- hobbies (activities like golf club memberships etc.)

- cost of parking

Flexible expenses also don't mean these things aren't necessary. The flexibility refers to the flexibility of the amount, not the importance of the item or service.

Allocate a Larger Portion to Fixed Expenses

This is where the 50/30/20 budget rule will really help you.

You can now set your budget up in such a way that most of the 50% for needs goes toward your fixed expenses. They are after all the most important bills and can't be skipped, and you are able to plan for them better.

Again, not all flexible expenses are unimportant, but you can always divide flexible expenses into categories of negotiable and non-negotiable expenses too. This is just to help you see which flexible expenses can be cut and which can't, as well as ensuring that your 50% is spent on the most urgent needs.

Only after this is done will you have a true idea of what can be used on the other flexible expenses.

Monitor and Adjust Expenses as Needed

Before you can reduce your expenses, you have to know what you're spending on fixed and flexible expenses. Take the time to look back and list all the recurring bills you get, subscriptions you're signed up to, and anything else that you know you pay day after day. Then have a look at what you buy daily or weekly that doesn't form part of your urgent expenses or that can't be predicted every single time you buy it.

You can now decide where to cut back on and what to get rid of entirely.

By monitoring and adjusting your expenses regularly, you stay ahead of your financial situation and you can prepare for difficult times better.

How to Stick to Your Budget and Adjust as Needed

Setting It Up

For people who don't know how to set up a budget it can seem difficult, so many don't even bother. But, setting up your budget involves three simple things.

- Taking down your income.

- Making a list of all your expenses.

- Implementing the 50/30/20 budget rule.

Remember that even with the 50/30/20 budget rule, if you have money left after paying all your bills, buying what you wanted, and putting the proper amounts into savings, you don't have to spend it on nonsense just because it's there.

The point of making the budget isn't to check how much money you can use on things you don't need after paying for the things you do need. It's about giving every penny a job.

And if you're lucky enough to have money left over, find something useful for it.

Sticking To It

Even if you've managed to get started with setting up your budget and it looks good on paper, the hard part is yet to come. This is the sticking to it part.

Here are some tips to help you stick to your budget.

- Be realistic. It's great that you're feeling inspired and want to save as much as you can, but telling yourself you will only eat at home every single month or you'll say no to every night out with your friends is just not realistic.

  Aside from deserving a reward for working hard for your money, you also can't deny that sometimes all you want to do is treat yourself, so be sure to set goals that you know you can achieve if you push yourself. Eating out once or twice a month is much more doable than not eating out at all.

- Budget for the following month. Don't budget for the month you're in because you can easily overlook certain things and that can throw off your calculations and mess everything up. If you're doing a monthly budget, be sure to budget for the next month in order to stay ahead and not be rushed.

- Auto-drafts are best. Auto drafts are set up with your bank and basically just means that bills that are fixed and to be paid the same time every month can be taken from your salary when it comes in and paid to whoever it should be paid to, without you having to keep remembering to log into your account and do it. It saves you time and energy, not to mention it ensures the bills are paid on time.

- Weekly allowance. It'll help to split your spending money over weeks. This will help to ensure you make it to the end of the month without running out, as you have an amount allocated to each week. It will also encourage you to buy only what's necessary.

- Avoid credit cards. There's no doubt that getting a large sum of money now and paying over time sounds fantastic, but this is just an **enabler** to spend money you don't have and often on things you don't need. Keep in mind that the money you're getting is always going to be less than what you're paying back (because of admin fees and interest), so why even bother? All you're doing is adding another expense to your budget.

- Say no to temptation. This is not going to be easy. Many people rely on instant **gratification** like **impulse** purchases to get over the stress of working all month, but trust me, it's not worth it. You often regret having bought it and it might cause more stress. If you really want something, you can always save for it and buy it when the time is right.

Stay Accountable and Track Progress

It's hard to stay accountable for spending, especially when you're single. This is why there are different ways to do so to ensure you are reminded of your goals and stay on track.

You can link your spending to your work to help in this regard.

As we spend the money we have, we don't even think of the amount of work that went into earning or bringing forth that money. That is why, if you link the amount of money you want to spend to the hours or days it took you to make that money, it might help you rethink your choices.

Is one pair of shoes really worth nearly 17 days of sweat and stress?

Furthermore, it will also do you good to find an **accountability** partner. This will be someone close to you whose opinions and advice you value, because it will be their responsibility to check in on your progress.

They will also have to encourage you to keep going and hold you accountable when you don't. These people remind you what you're working towards and even when you have moments when you fail to stick to the budget, they help you see why continuing is better than quitting.

Tracking your progress means to record every single penny you spend. If you bought something at Starbucks today, record it. If your colleagues are having a group night out this month and you weren't planning to go but ended up there, record it.

Doing so will help you see where you already used up any funds for entertainment and it will help you be more **mindful** until the budget resets.

Celebrate Small Wins

You may think celebrating small wins seems **counterproductive**, but I assure you it helps with staying motivated. Maintaining good financial habits is a skill and doesn't come without sacrifice, which is why we should reward these sacrifices from time to time.

Sure, you're budgeting because you want to reach certain goals and these goals form part of the reward, but the fact that you're able to live the life you want and create a future you can look forward to is something you should continuously reward yourself for. You don't have to go overboard with the celebrations but as long as you do it, you'll want to keep pushing forward.

A small win might be sticking to home-cooked meals for three months and the reward for this could be eating at your favorite restaurant the month after.

Implementing fun and rewards into this process will make it feel like less of a burden.

Chapter 3:
Saving Money

I used to say why save money if I'll die tomorrow, I haven't died yet and I have nothing to survive on. –Bangambiki Habyarimana

I think the **vast** majority of people feel that saving money has little value, because you don't know if you'll live to see the day when you'd actually need it, but what many don't think about is what to do when you do live to see that day.

What happens when you've been earning good money for 20—30 years without giving saving some of that money a second thought, and suddenly, your life gets turned upside down? Do you have family and friends who can bail you out of any financial crisis you face? The answer to this is likely no, since everyone nowadays is trying to get by too.

If nothing else can convince you, this thought should. No one wants to work their whole life establishing the lifestyle they've always wanted only for one thing to go wrong and strip them of everything they have.

Unfortunately, this happens all too often and the main reason for this is a lack of savings.

Understanding the Importance of Saving Money

Let's discuss some of the **fundamentals** surrounding saving money.

Psychology

Did you know that saving money can have an amazing effect on your mood and mental well-being? It's true.

When you think about it, it makes sense because never having enough money to get through the month or struggling to pay bills can cause a huge amount of stress. So, **evidently**, having a successful savings plan and proper budget in place reduces that stress.

The level of peace of mind a person has when their finances are in order leads to a happier life. These kinds of people have a positive attitude towards life, its challenges, and can better handle stress when it arises. This is not to say people with savings don't feel stressed or unhappy, but it's likely for very different reasons than money problems.

Permanent or persistent financial instability can cause a person to be in a constant state of stress which negatively affects their mental health, as well as their physical health.

I know some people who've actually been close to nervous breakdowns because they couldn't lower their anxiety and stress levels caused by their financial circumstances. They felt lost because they didn't know how or where to begin, and the stress consumed them. This is an extremely dangerous headspace to be in, because in some of the worst cases, mental strain to such an extent can lead to self-harm and substance abuse.

Saving for Short-Term and Long-Term

While saving is important, it's best to know what you're saving for and the timeframe of each savings plan. You develop better discipline when you know the kind of approach each type of savings requires.

Short-term goals, as you know, are the kind of savings you have for fun things or items you want to buy. It can also be your emergency fund, because you'll be able to access that money quicker.

Your long-term goals on the other hand, will be those big dreams you have to work much harder towards and save much longer to make up the necessary money.

It's easy to make the mistake of keeping your entire savings in one place and then using from there as the needs arise, but this may not always be the best option. Not only because it's better to have the funds you can spend now and the funds for later kept separately, but also because of the different benefits specific savings accounts offer.

Take your time to do research on the different kinds of savings accounts and decide which is best for you from there. Keep your eye out for the relevant interest rates, **minimum** balances, risks, additional fees, admin fees, and waiting periods to collect those funds.

You don't want to think you can keep your short-term savings with the long-term savings and when you go to withdraw, you're told you can't withdraw until a specific amount of time has passed.

Federal Deposit Insurance Corporation-insured (FDIC) deposit accounts would be a better option for accounts where money will need to be accessed as soon as possible. It can be a general savings account or certificate of deposit (CD). Although CD accounts secures funds for a certain period, the rates on these accounts are usually higher in comparison to general savings accounts.

In the case of long-term savings, you should look at investment accounts through broker-dealers, or tax-efficient accounts like 529 plans and IRAs (retirement funds).

Impact of Inflation

In most cases, the demand for goods and services is the driving force behind the increase of prices. This is inflation and although there are many other factors that also affect inflation, the majority of these factors have minimal range and are quite brief.

For instance, weather conditions might affect the production and harvest of certain crops and cause farmers to increase their prices temporarily.

This is then reflected at supermarkets when consumers are also expected to pay more. The price of different goods and services is monitored by The Consumer Price Index (CPI), and this information is made available to the public monthly.

Protecting Your Savings

Inflation is unavoidable; however, there are ways to protect your savings.

Investments allow you to get better returns in **contrast** to simply placing it into savings accounts or money markets. That said, you need to be aware of the risks involved when investing because investments present more risks than an account that has been FDIC-insured.

Many people go for stock investments as a more well-known way to get around inflation; however, as with everything, you need to educate yourself on the specific stock you're planning to invest in. This is to ensure you choose the best-suited options for your personal goals rather than following everyone else.

Precious metals, like copper, silver, or gold, are also good options for investments.

The Importance of Safety Nets

Safety nets are **crucial** in times of emergencies and I'm not only talking about when you unexpectedly lose your job or encounter an accident. Pay-cuts, natural disasters, pandemics, and sudden changes in your health are all emergencies because you're unable to predict it. A safety net helps you get through these emergencies easier since a large part of the strain is financial. And since most of us don't have the funds to tackle such major disruptions readily available, it's better to put money away monthly in case of a rainy day.

Building Wealth Over Time

For those who don't only want to have money in their pockets but also build wealth, saving is essential. Long-term wealth is primarily achieved through investments. Not that your money can't grow in savings accounts, but the most effective and steadiest way to maximize your returns would be by investing.

Achieving Long-Term Financial Goals

Long-term financial goals mostly spark thoughts of buying a new car, continuing your studies, or buying a house, but for a lot of people buying a new furnace or refrigerator falls into this category too.

It might be because they have too much debt so their bills amount to more than their income, or their income is just not enough to put big amounts into savings. This means that while one person saves five to ten years for a new house, another saves for a new home appliance or what have you.

And yes, credit cards or micro loans are also possible, but why get yourself into more debt when you can save up for the thing you need?

Creating a Savings Plan

It's common for people to think that a budget and savings plan is the same thing; however, they have key differences.

Yes, both help in achieving financial goals but have slightly different functions. In a nutshell, a budget helps you manage your daily spending whereas savings plans are used to develop a steady financial blueprint that enables you to reach your life goals. Savings plans also ensure you make provision for setbacks and emergencies that can occur at any point in your life.

Regardless of their differences, neither one has to be the headache people make them out to be. Budgets tend to need a review of income and expenses frequently, usually monthly, while savings plans can be reviewed quarterly or twice a year.

S.M.A.R.T: Specific, Measurable, Achievable, Relevant and Time Bound

Unlike general savings, setting a S.M.A.R.T goal means you allocate a specific amount and time period to a specific goal.

The S.M.A.R.T goal can be better understood when broken up:

S—Specific. Refers to knowing exactly what you're saving for.

M—Measurable. Refers to the goal allowing room for you to establish how long it'll take to achieve.

A—Achievable. Means exactly what it says, it is not impossible to achieve.

R—Relevant. It needs to be something you won't easily lose interest in so it has to be relevant to you.

T—Time bound. Refers to setting a sort of deadline for yourself to achieve it by.

If you'd like to take a week vacation, whether abroad or locally, set a S.M.A.R.T goal to save for it. You can figure out how much is needed to save and how long you'll need to save to make up the necessary money.

Of course, these goals have to be realistically achievable in the time you're giving yourself to save for it, so most S.M.A.R.T goals depend highly on the goal itself and the money you have available to be placed into savings for it each month.

Determining the Amount

Having an ultimate goal is already a great start to beginning a positive financial journey, but breaking it up into smaller goals makes it that much easier to do and offers more noticeable results in the short-term.

The human brain finds difficulty choosing delayed gratification (rewards at a later stage, over instant gratification (rewards right now). This means working tirelessly toward the ultimate goal without having anything to show for it in the meantime can **foster** feelings of pointlessness and you're likely to end up losing faith in the process.

For this reason, it is recommended to set smaller goals as you go along.

These goals can even be weekly savings because the main goal becomes more manageable when you're actively seeing the small amounts grow to big ones. It has a clear impact on your attitude and confidence.

The way to find out how much your savings should be is to establish how much you need for the item you want. Sometimes the amounts may be small so you'd only have to save for a few months and other times the amount may be significant and you'd have to save all the way into the following year.

This is still alright because you know what you're working towards.

Now that you know how much the item costs, figure out how long you will have to save if you put a reasonable amount consistently towards it. Be sure to be honest with yourself about how much you have available for this and you're not going to end up saving $25 dollars one week and then $5 the next.

Once you know how long you'll have to save to comfortably gather the total, divide that total by the number of weeks you think it'll take. The amount you're left with is going to be your target figure. The target figure is what you're going to aim to put away weekly towards this S.M.A.R.T goal.

If you notice you're expected to save more than you have available to save weekly, have a look at your budget and see if there's anywhere you'd be able to cut costs, even if it's only for the number of weeks that you'll be saving for your S.M.A.R.T goal to be accomplished.

Choosing Savings Account That Fit Your Needs

Everyone has different priorities, and everyone's financial situation allows room for different things.

This is why it's important to ensure the savings accounts you choose are in line with your personal needs. Your friend or family member may have suggested one that works great for them but then a few months into your savings you notice that you're not happy with how the interest is growing or whatever else.

It's because of the difference in needs and wants, that we have to be mindful of the fact that something that works for someone else might not work for us.

Do proper research about the kind of savings account that is best suited to you because, while savings accounts are pretty straightforward, they don't all share the same features. Some may require higher deposits while others need a minimum balance to remain in the account. The most suitable accounts; however, are those with the highest interest rates and least requirements.

Some things to look for when choosing a savings account are:

- **Required minimum balance**—Minimum balances are the lowest amounts allowed in an account. Anything less than it will result in additional fees being charged. You want to look for an account that is the most reasonable with its minimum balance requirements.

- **Rate tiers**—The tiers refer to the **criteria** needed to earn a certain rate of interest on your savings. The best thing would be to find savings accounts that don't have a long list of criteria to meet to earn good interest.

- **Opening deposit**—This is common with the majority of finance companies. You need to pay a deposit when opening the account. The fees vary but of course, you should look for ones in your affordability range.

- **Accessibility**—Since you will use these funds at random times, you don't want an account with limited access. Find out how easy it will be to withdraw your money from that account and how regular withdrawals will affect it.

- **Account fees**—All accounts have fees. They could be monthly or annual fees, **penalties** for when the balance is low or when your account is inactive for a while. Understand what these fees are and how they'll affect your savings plan.

Automate Your Savings With Direct Deposit or Automatic Transfers

Direct Deposits and automatic transfers are technically the same thing. It means you set up an arrangement with your bank or employer to deposit a portion of your income into your savings account with each paycheck you receive. The remainder will then go to your checking account which is what you will use to pay bills and buy goods.

People go for this method because it makes it easier to save, since you don't risk forgetting to deposit it yourself or depositing late and **incurring** additional fees. You will also stand a better chance of saving money every month because you don't even have a chance to change your mind. As soon as it enters your account, it'll be transferred into savings.

That way you are forced to make do with what you're left with.

Understanding the Power of Compounding and How to Maximize It

Basically, compound interest is interest earned on top of savings that has already earned interest. At first the amounts appear small and not quite worth it, but as you allow that money to remain in the account and grow interest, the speed at which the interest is grown increases rapidly. Meaning the higher the balance in the account, the higher the interest you earn will be.

You can maximize compound interest in the following ways.

- Start as soon as possible. As you can see, the longer your money remains in the account, the more interest it gains. The interest automatically increases the balance which in turn increases the compound interest.

  That's why the sooner you start, the sooner you'll be able to start accumulating interest and rapidly growing the initial amount you put into savings. This is not to say you shouldn't keep adding monthly **contributions** to the savings account and rely solely on the balance you put in to begin with to do all the heavy lifting. Be sure to keep adding to that amount and you'll be shocked to see that number rise in the coming years.

- Choose accounts that compound monthly or quarterly, rather than annually. With the **principle** of simple interest earning compound interest, it only makes sense that the more often your balance compounds, the quicker it'll increase. Annual compound still makes a difference to your balance, but it won't yield the same results as monthly or quarterly compounds.

- Don't be stingy with how much you put into the account. Just because there is a minimum you need to put into the account doesn't mean you should stick to that. If you have more than needed available, why not add it to the savings?

  The more you put into the savings account, the more you'll get out of it. It will also allow you to grow the money quicker than waiting for it to compound only on the little that's there.

- Find rewards accounts. Many banks have special offers for people who meet a particular criterion. Most of these offers involve higher interest rates if you swipe your debit card a number of times monthly, but it's **imperative** that you first assess if the requirements are worth the rise in interest. You might be better off sticking to what you have.

- Find out if you belong to a specific group of people who might be offered an additional special. This is particularly the case for military members and younger people. It can't hurt to ask and many banks do in fact have **initiatives** where they give young people higher interest rates in order to **encourage** saving early.

- Look for new-customer deals. More often than not, banks are holding specials for new customers to bring business in, so don't be shy to ask if they have any current new-customer specials. It may be lowered account fees, higher interests, or other discounts on fees to motivate customers to bank with them.

- Check with multiple places. You might be sold on something a consultant made look like a must-have but be sure not to settle for the first bank you speak to. Do a bit of shopping at different financial institutions and compare the information and benefits.

Thereafter, you can make a well-informed decision.

Make Use of Apps and Websites to Support Your Saving Efforts

There are different reasons why people prefer using banking apps to help them manage their finances than rely on their own memory. The evolution of technology prioritizes the user's needs as the primary focus, so why not take advantage of it?

Banking apps make our lives so much easier by helping keep our bills organized, improve our budgeting methods, and offer advice and recommendations of best suited goods and services. The **algorithms** on our personal devices are designed to feed us the information we desperately need, sometimes without having to actively seek it out.

Familiarize yourself with financial apps and websites so you can control your money with confidence and ease.

Chapter 4:
Investing Money

If you aren't thinking about owning a stock for ten years, don't even think about owning it for ten minutes. –Warren Buffett

Investments and investing can seem like such a drag and the terms used in this sector are confusing and outright boring, especially if you're just starting out. It could be why so many people decide to just drop the whole idea, because there's too many big words to remember and who has time for that?

The answer is very few people, but trust me those who do, end up reaping the rewards of their efforts. That's why I'm going to take you on a slow walk through the reality of investing, its benefits, and more, so that you can see just how simple it is.

Understanding the Different Types of Investments

Even though this is an ever-growing sector, once you educate yourself on how it works and what to look for, it becomes much easier. You have to understand that all investments come with their own risks and while there are many that are ideal for newcomers, there are also plenty that call for a solid understanding of the ins-and-outs of how this sector functions.

Having the necessary knowledge is only to protect you from biting off more than you can chew or making bad choices that can cost you loads of money. Any advice you follow should be from a **seasoned** investor or financial professional.

The most common ways to buy different types of investments is through a financial advisor or by setting up an online **brokerage account**.

Financial advisors make the getting into the buying-and-trading world easier and guide you on a safe but secure financial path.

Brokerage accounts can either be opened directly by you or with the help of a financial advisor. This account makes it possible to purchase mutual funds, bonds, stocks, etc. Something about brokerage accounts you should be careful of, is the fact that the final decisions are yours to make so it's important that you know what you're doing.

Here are some of the different types of investments:

- **Mutual funds**—Think of this as an investment that multiple other investors are also investing in. You all throw your money into the same pot and the portfolio manager sends that money to different kinds of investments like bonds or stocks. These investments have a minimum starting amount, so you'd have to put a certain amount in to begin.

  The higher the amount you put in, the more you'll get compared to someone who puts in less.

  Mutual funds can be passive, meaning you don't have to check and manage it all the time, but this can increase your chances of overlooking a failing investment. They can also be active, meaning there's someone to monitor it all the time, like a portfolio manager, but you might end up having to pay more than expected because you'll also be paying for that person to keep an eye on your investment.

- **Real estate**—This type involves buying commercial and residential properties. A commercial property is a property that will be used to run a business from, you can either rent it out or sell it, and a residential property is one that functions as a home and can also be rented out or sold.

If being a **landlord** sounds like too much to begin with, you can always buy shares in real estate. It's almost like a mutual fund but in the real estate sector, commonly known as real estate investment trusts (REITS).

- **Commodities**—As you know, commodities are physical goods such as precious metals like copper, gold, and silver, or any other **agricultural** product of value. You can either find out about commodity pools or search for private investment channels like "managed futures fund" (Chen, n.d., p.18). These kinds of funds also act similar to mutual funds.

The more money you invest in funds like these, the higher your personal risks are.

- **Stocks**—Here, you're going to be buying a share of a company's wealth. If the company does well, then your stocks grow, but if it does poorly, then your stocks drop. Even though you own a share of the company's wealth, you don't actually own the company. That said, if the company closes down for some reason, owning stocks means you get to claim your share.

Additionally, most stocks pay portions to investors quarterly, but there are some who pay monthly.

- **Bonds**—This involves loaning money to a borrower. There are always fixed interest rates added to the loan amounts, and this is what the lender makes in exchange for the borrower using their money.

Long-Term vs Short-Term Investments

Long-term investments refer to those you have for over a year. Whether it's bonds, real estate, or stocks, it needs to be on your profile for longer than a year to be seen as a long-term investment.

Short-term investments are those on your portfolio for a year or less. Holding an investment for less than a year usually means the investor is more interested in buying and selling, and isn't using these short-term investments to build his long-term financial portfolio.

Active vs Passive Investments

Active

Active investments are ideal for people who have the time to check and manage it regularly. Whether you hire a portfolio manager or manage the investment personally, someone has to keep their eye on an active investment. Also, whoever is actively managing this investment has to know exactly what they are doing, because it'll be their job to choose when the best time is to buy or sell.

They also have to know which assets will get you the highest return.

Pros

- Tax management. Tax is **inescapable** but with the necessary knowledge and skills you could find or create strategies to reduce the burden of taxes, like selling failing investments to cover those costs.

- Flexibility. Since there's no strict index to follow you can go ahead and buy those assets you believe to be hidden gems without any problems.

- Hedging. **Hedging** means to protect your investments and this can be done by making use of **short-sales** or exiting when you foresee increasing risks, or if the risk is too significant.

Cons

- Higher risk. Having the freedom of buying any investment you have faith in can become a problem when what you thought you'd get doesn't match what you're getting. You stand to lose much more than you put in.

- Pricey. The estimated average expense is higher on active investments, because of the extra funds going into it, like transaction fees for continuous buying-and-selling and salaries (if you hired people to manage your investments).

Passive

Typically chosen for its long-term benefits, passive investments are also cheaper to invest in, because you're not going to be buying and selling every few weeks or months. Even when it seems like a great idea to sell the asset, passive investing requires the discipline to buy-and-keep, until it is smart to sell.

Pros

- Tax efficiency. Your capital gains tax will be less because you're not selling all year round.

- Lower fees. These investments follow an index which means you don't have to hire anyone to monitor the progress.

- Straightforward. The index acts as a guideline of which asset is in the fund and how well it is performing. That means you don't have to figure out or manually compare how the investment is progressing.

Cons

- Lower returns. Since these investments are designed to match the market. Returns are rarely massive. There are times that they go slightly above the market but it will never be as much as with active investments.

- Limited. Indexes have very specific investments so variety is not an option here.

The Benefits of Investing

Build Wealth

Be sure that you know what you want and by which point of your life you want it, because this will be the best way to help decide which of the many investment options are right for you. Even if you don't have a lot of money to put into investing right now, know that no matter how hard it is to put bits from the little you have away, it'll be worth it in the end.

Especially now when you may not have any serious responsibilities, you can set yourself up for a great future.

Long-Term Returns

Investing your money can look like you're risking way more than you'll actually get out, but not knowing if the investment will grow or fall causes this fear. You can't let fear stop you because one thing's for sure, you will never be able to find out if that investment can grow your money without trying. Not all assets will cost you all or nothing, but you have to be willing to take the chance in order to find out.

Asset prices that rise and fall can even be used to your benefit, since you will then be able to buy them for next-to-nothing and potentially get bigger returns later down the line.

Protection From Inflation

You've already seen how inflation can kill the value of your money, so not investing it could actually be seen as losing money. Investing your money can help you beat this monster because your returns are constantly increasing, meaning as long as your returns are higher than inflation, you don't have to worry.

Understanding Risk and Reward

Risk and rewards are calculated in the form of a **ratio** when it comes to investments and is used to help understand whether a specific asset is worth it. The reward refers to the potential "reward an investor can earn for every dollar they risk" (Hayes, n.d., p.1).

This is super important to the process because it will help you calculate how much returns you can get and what the needed risk for that return will be.

An example of how the risk-reward ratio works is as follows: If it's 1:9, it means that for every $1 you risk, you could potentially earn $9. Most investors don't feel confident in such high rewards and find the safest risk-rewards ratio to be 1:3.

As a beginner, your best bet is to get advice from a financial professional before investing in assets with greater risks or unusually high rewards. Once you've gotten more experience and increased your knowledge, you will have the confidence to make these decisions on your own.

Diversifying Your Investment Portfolio

First let me explain what a financial portfolio is before I ramble on about why diversifying it is good for you.

This is the group of financial investments a person has under their name. Your portfolio can have different kinds of investments listed like real estate, stocks, and bonds. Every investor has a financial portfolio even if you've only bought one type of asset, and while you can manage your own portfolio, it's often best to get the help of a professional.

Diversifying your portfolio means to invest in different assets because of the uncertainty of the future and finance markets. If one investment does poorly, you'll still have others to fall back on. Yearly review of your portfolio will help you make the best decisions for diversification and ensure that all your goals are not depending on the performance on only one investment.

Is It Possible to Over-Diversify?

As with everything in life, too much of a good thing can be bad, so yes, it is possible to go overboard with diversification. Sometimes people invest in assets that don't even add noticeable benefits to their portfolio and end up wasting money on unnecessary assets. Therefore, you should be careful to not get caught up in trying to create a diverse portfolio to the extent that you're buying investments all over the place, but they don't add any value to your financial journey.

Also, the hunger to have a perfectly diverse portfolio can sometimes confuse people and they end up buying more than one fund in the same investment type, which is obviously not adding diversity. It simply means you're investing in the same type of asset, only through multiple funds. A proper example of what a diverse portfolio looks like is investments in bonds, real estate, mutual funds, and commodities.

Now that is a diverse portfolio.

The Back-Bone of a Diversified Portfolio

What I mean by back-bone of a diversified portfolio, is the investments you can expect to have the most impact on your portfolio. Having one or two of these as well as smaller investments can make for an exceptional portfolio.

- **Bonds**—Due to the consistent interest bonds earn, they are very reliable investments.

- **International stocks**—Stocks outside the US perform differently to those inside the US. Additionally, you may have access to opportunities that aren't available in the US. Still, remember that foreign stocks can come with higher risks because of such high returns, so be prepared for that.

- **Domestic stocks**—This option offers higher growth in the long-run, but at the same time comes with increased short-term risks. Stocks **fluctuate** more than any other asset, so depending on the value of your stock at the time you want to sell, you might sit with a stock that's worth less than what you initially paid for it.

- **Short-term investments**—Money-market funds and CDs (mentioned earlier in the book) fall into this category. Even though money-market funds are seen as lower risk and offer greater levels of stability, the returns are lower than that of bonds. The security these funds offer, unfortunately, come at the cost of high returns.

With all these options available to you, all you have to do is ask a professional for help to get started and which options are best for your personal goals. Savings and investments don't have to start when you're already paying a bunch of bills; jump at the opportunity while you're still young and barely have money problems, to protect yourself from a financially **crippling** future.

Chapter 5:
Credit, Debit, Cash Flow

Making more money will not solve your problems if cash flow management is your problem. –Robert Kiyosaki

You've been given quite a chunk of information that may seem tough to remember, but is definitely worth thinking about. But what about the actual **definitions**, uses, and benefits, of the main kinds of financial transactions? Do you know how each one affects your account?

Don't stress that's exactly what I plan to help you with in this chapter.

Defining Credit, Debit, and Cash Flow

It must be tiring having to learn all these terms, but I assure you, you're going to be glad you did.

Why, you ask? Because the financial world has plenty of **jargon,** and a lot of the time people get themselves into a mess because they don't understand half of it.

So, let's jump right in.

Credit

Credits into an account refers to money being paid that increases that account's balance. It is paid in by either an employer or someone you know electronically; however, it's possible to pay it directly into your account through an ATM.

Debit

Debits represent money being taken from an account which causes a decrease in the balance. This can be monthly car bills, mortgage and rental payments, etc.

Both of these transactions can be found when you draw an account statement, so you'll be able to see every penny that leaves your account and where it's gone, or where it came from.

Cash Flow

This is exactly what it sounds like: The flow of cash. It refers to the cyber travel (so to speak), of money. Inflow describes how money flows into a specific account, and outflow describes how money flows out of an account.

Understanding Credit and How It Works

Credit isn't only used to describe the money that is paid into an account, it can also refer to money that is lent to you by a financial service provider. This is done by approaching a bank or financial institution with a request for a certain amount of money you'd like to borrow, and they will then use all the documents and information you provide them to see if they can offer you that amount and if you will be able to pay.

They use your total monthly income and expenses as a way to determine how likely it is for you to pay, and once you are successful, your account is credited. To make this possible, you will have to sign an agreement stating how long you will be expected to pay and how much you will be paying to them monthly, to repay that debt.

It's essential that you understand and read through every document before signing, because some companies have extremely high interest rates and you might be able to get the same for cheaper elsewhere.

The interest is, of course, the profit the lender makes on loaning you money, but they will probably mention other costs like admin, service, and late fees too.

How It Works

As explained above, when you apply for credit, you are basically asking a financial institute to give you a certain amount of money now, and then you agree to pay them back monthly (with all their added fees) over a specific amount of time. This is a legal agreement and has different names like credit agreement or loan contract, but mean the same thing.

The agreement lists a range of things and should be read carefully and should not be rushed. You want to know exactly what you are getting yourself into, because you can't simply refuse to pay once you have signed. Failing to adhere to your agreement can result in legal action being taken against you which is why it's so important to know what you are signing.

The main points found in the agreement include the repayment amount and duration, interest rates, credit that was given to you, any conditions you have to continue to meet until the end of your agreement, and what the consequences will be if you don't meet these conditions. Just like with your bank account, you can draw a statement monthly for credit agreements to see how much you have paid and what is left on that agreement.

Just remember that everyone knows how unpredictable life can be, so there are options to take insurance on some credit agreements in the event that you somehow become unable to pay. If you have the money to add this on, it is highly recommended.

Different Types of Credit

The two main forms in which credit is offered is as *revolving credit* or *installment credit*.

- **Revolving credit**—Refers to credit that can be borrowed over and over again. Meaning you can withdraw from the total credit you want gradually, so you don't have to use it all at once. Most people prefer this, because even when they pay only the installments (not the full sum of credit they were given), they can borrow a portion of that money again. If the full credit has been paid, the revolving credit agreement doesn't come to an end. Instead, it remains available for you to use again. Still, this cycle of continuous borrowing can be tough in the long-run, since you'll practically never be done paying unless you stop using it or cancel.

- **Installment credit**—Is when you get the full amount of money you want to borrow paid into your account. You then make arrangements to pay it back monthly and for a certain number of months or years. There is no way to use any of the money again, even when making monthly repayments, and the agreement comes to an end when everything has been paid back. Bigger loans like student loans, personal loans, and mortgages are usually installment credits.

Don't forget that interest rates will always apply. This is because that is what the financial institution earns from loaning you the money. Every situation is unique, so you won't know beforehand exactly what the interest rate they'll charge you will be.

Different companies have different rates and there are other things that also affect the rate you're charged, like your credit history, income, risk assessment, and the company's policies itself.

Just be sure to check for that so that you know how much of your monthly repayment goes to the company and how much goes toward paying off the balance.

The Benefits and Risks of Using Credit

As great as it sounds to get a large sum of money now and pay it back later, there are a few important things you have to know. Life is all about weighing the pros and cons of something, so let's do that.

Pros of using credit:

- The convenience of getting your hands on large sums of money now and only paying later on.

- Some cards offer protection on the things you buy (so if what you bought with the credit gets stolen during a certain period, you can be **refunded** or the item can be replaced).

- Can be used to build a good credit history and score.

- Perfect in times of emergencies.

Cons of using credit:

- Borrowing unsurprisingly increases your debt.

- Can damage credit history and score if used incorrectly.

- Losing lots of money to additional fees and interest rates.

- Going overboard with spending.

Know Your Credit History and Score

You may be wondering why a credit history and credit score is important to begin with. Well, if you want to borrow money from a financial institution, the first thing they'll do is check these two things. While the two are related to each other, and the credit history affects the credit score, they are not the same thing.

Credit History

Your credit history comes in the form of a statement and lists every type of credit agreement you've ever had. Even the ones that have been paid in full come up on this document. This document also has sensitive information about you on it, like your identification info and which companies you have active credit with, so you can't say you have no debt because they'll have a look at your history and see any accounts you still owe money on. The credit history helps them determine if they can offer you any more money and how much.

Credit Score

This score is made of three numbers and is usually between 300-850. It is the indicator of what kind of risk you are to the company lending you money. The higher your score, the less of a risk you are. This score is also used to see what the chances are of you paying your debt every month and on time.

Building and Maintaining a Good Credit Score

Things That Affect Your Credit Score

In the US, TransUnion, Experian, and Equifax are the main companies that compile your credit history. The information in the report is what is used to give you your credit score.

This includes:

- How long you have your credit agreements.

- Type of credit you have.

- How well you're paying it monthly.

- How much you still owe.

- Are there any new credit agreements to be added?

Steps to Build and Maintain a Good Credit Score

Before I tell you how to build and maintain a good credit score, understand that even though this information seems too personal for the banks to want, they have the right to know this. This is only to protect themselves from lending money to people who already have a bunch of bills to pay monthly, or who just don't care to pay their debt.

Put yourself in the bank's position; if you knew someone was going to take your money and never pay you back, would you still loan them money?

It's also for your own good because if the money you get monthly is already not enough to pay your bills, or just about enough, someone has to stop you from getting yourself into even more debt.

Now, let's get to the part where you learn to build and maintain a good score.

- Don't take on too much debt. The amount of people you owe counts greatly towards your credit score, so be sure not to open accounts or get credit from anywhere you can. Having too much debt will automatically lower your score.

- Pay your debt on time every month. This is another one of the major factors that can make or break your credit score. Paying on time shows that you manage your money responsibly and will make companies want to offer you money, because they can see you have no problems with paying.

Debt can be a good thing, since it can encourage financial institutions to give you more debt. But this can only be done if you pay them what you owe on time and don't have too many random debts outstanding.

Other Negatives That Affect Your Score

Aside from what I mentioned above, there are also smaller factors that impact your score. These are the diversity of your accounts, if you've applied for credit recently, and the period you have your debt for.

So, what does this mean? Let me explain each one in a bit more detail.

The diversity of your accounts means what different types of credit do you have. Do you only have credit cards? Or do you only have loans? Having different types of credit improves your score significantly.

But how does applying for credit lower your score? One application every six months or so won't do much harm, but if you're constantly trying to get credit at places every few weeks or months, you come across as overeager. For example, say you really want a girlfriend or boyfriend, so you try your luck every week or two to see if you'll get lucky. Rumors will spread and people will start thinking you're desperate, right?

Well, the same goes for credit.

Going around trying to get lucky every few months reflects poorly on you and lowers your credit score.

And finally, the period you have your debt for is so important to your score too. This is because banks would rather loan money to someone who values loyalty and will be a long-term customer, rather than someone who jumps from company-to-company. Even if you pay the credit in full, if you don't have to cancel your credit card and don't have to pay extra fees to keep it open, leaving it on your credit record will improve your score.

The Importance of Paying Bills on Time and Avoiding Debt

There are many benefits of paying your bills on time. You've seen how it can affect your credit score and credit history, but it's generally just a good way to have control over your finances. There can be serious consequences when you don't pay your bills on time. Even if you think it's no big deal when you're young, don't be surprised ten years down the line when you want to buy a house and you're reminded of that time in your life when you didn't bother paying your debt when you were supposed to.

It can really delay your plans and getting back on track with a history like that can be extremely difficult.

Here are some ways that paying your bills on time and not taking on too much debt can help you.

- **Less stress**—Yep, this comes up a lot. If you ever wondered why adults seem so serious all the time, it's stress. Most of the time it's financial stress. This is one of the major benefits of paying your bills on time, which may seem silly now, but as you get older and understand the way of the world, you'll learn that reducing stress wherever you can is a main selling point. Once you miss a payment, interest rates accumulate on that account and even when you make the next payment, you first have to pay the interest before the money will go to the remaining balance. So, just pay on time and you'll save yourself the headache.

- **No more late fees**—Another fee to be paid before money goes to the balance when you pay late. There are companies that'll charge you this fee even if you pay only a few hours later, and there's no getting upset about it either. This is likely mentioned in your credit agreement so you can't argue with it. Keep in mind that this is their business and whenever they can get extra money out of you, they will. Avoid this problem by paying on time.

- **Access to more**—Having little debt and a good payment history opens doors you can't even imagine. That business you always wanted to open can now become a reality because for five years you've only had good debt and been paying on time every single month. Banks will jump at the chance to offer you money because they have evidence that you are a good investment.

Other benefits of this habit include lower interest rates which can lead to lower installments. You don't get flagged as a high risk so financial companies will be more willing to offer you good deals.

Understanding Debit Cards and Electronic Payment Methods

A debit card is linked to your check account, so every purchase you make gets deducted from that money. Most debit cards also have protection on your purchases, which is great in times when the item you bought is faulty.

A credit card is one that is issued by a finance company and contains the funds you have borrowed. These accounts usually have interests and higher additional fees.

Electronic payments involve any type of payment that is done digitally, meaning you don't have to have actual cash to make the purchase. Again, there are pros and cons to using this service.

Pros include

- Lower transaction fees. This doesn't necessarily mean the fees for electronic payments are lower than making payments in cash, but since making cash payments means you have to physically go to the stores to pay it, it could cost you more to get there compared to just paying it electronically. Even if you choose to pay by check, you could be looking at postage fees.

- Convenient and quick. Being able to shop from the comfort of your bed is truly one of the things that make electronic payments so much better. You can buy something on the other side of the world with a few clicks on your phone or computer.

- Reduced safety risk of carrying money. Crime is a major concern when you have large, or sometimes any amount really, of money on you. You stand a bigger chance of being mugged when you carry cash, which is why a lot of people prefer keeping their money safely in accounts.

Cons include

- Risk of **unauthorized** transactions. Since all your payment details are online and cyber-crime is a real thing, you risk being hacked and someone on the other side of the world making transactions without your consent. This can be tough to resolve and can take a long time to get your money back, if you're lucky enough to get it back.

- Higher cost for online security. Since cyber-crime is such a real risk, you'd want to protect your funds at all costs. Especially when you start investing and growing the money linked to your personal information. That means that you may have to pay higher fees for systems that can protect your sensitive data.

- Identity theft and general hacking. As you can see, the main concern with electronic payments is cyber-crime. Technology is so advanced that, with the right skills, someone can hack into your private accounts and extract all your personal details and use them without your knowledge or consent. This is why setting up **complex** cyber security systems is vital for the protection of your data. Many people feel it's not worth the risk so they steer clear from electronic payments as much as they can, but ultimately the decision is yours. Times are changing and it's often best to change with it.

Ways you can protect your sensitive data is to:

- Keep an eye out for phishing. This is usually done through sending fake emails to people, convincing them to click on unreliable links to "protect them." When actually those links are what opens the door to be hacked. If you don't recognize the email or anything seems off, rather delete it immediately.

- Make sure the passwords you set are as strong as possible. You might think it's easier to make all your passwords the same and easy-to-remember, but it's important that you make it as complicated as you can. Also, be sure to change passwords often, so you don't input the same one too many times.

- Update all your electronic devices with proper security systems regularly. The updates are designed to fix any security **vulnerabilities** found and act as another layer of protection.

- Avoid sending money to people you don't know. Make sure the person you're sending money to has a valid account and they are **credible** sources.

- Https sites only. These sites are **encrypted** and have their own level of protection from hackers, so be sure to check the top of your browser for the https and the padlock. It means that the site you're on is secure and minimizes your risks. As much as you want those sneakers or that bag, it's just not worth it if the site is not secure.

- Use only verified services to share sensitive information like account numbers. Emails may seem safe but trust me, it's not. Even sharing it via phone call is safer than sharing it via email.

- Use two-step verifications for more protection. This might be a bit annoying at first, but you'll be doing yourself a huge favor. The two-step verification usually involves entering your password and then having a code sent to your cell.

Cash Flow and How to Manage It

Cashflow, as mentioned earlier, is the way money flows in and out of your account. Positive cash flow means that the money flowing into your account is more than the money flowing out.

This is a great reflection on your financial habits.

Cash inflow can be any money coming into your account, whether from your salary, investments, or wherever. Cash outflow can be any money going out of your account, whether for bills or simply fees.

You can manage this flow by ensuring your outflow isn't higher than your inflow. Also, invest in assets with positive returns coming in regularly. You should also

check your statements often, to review your cash flow
and see where costs can be reduced.

Chapter 6:
Cost-of-Living

Everything costs something. –Zara Hairston

While the definition of the cost-of-living is simple, there are different factors that are used to determine what the actual cost-of-living in a particular area and era is.

Taxes, food, housing, transportation, and more, all form the basis of how the cost-of-living is calculated. All major verified companies provide data regarding what the cost of basic needs in a certain place is. Places like the Department of Housing and Urban Development and the US Food and Drug Administration are an example of the type of organizations providing the necessary data.

Let's discuss the primary factors that influence an area's cost of living.

- **Housing**—An area's cost-of-living depends on a lot of things; however, housing is one of the significant factors. Housing also doesn't only refer to the mortgage fees. It also involves property taxes, utility fees, maintenance fees, and homeowners' association fees, among others.

- **Family expenses**—This refers to expenses like school or day-care. Schooling expenses for older kids are usually lower than that of younger children, since they don't need as much care and attention.

- **Transportation**—: It goes without saying that this depends highly on how far from your home you work, and what mode of transport you use. For people who drive their own car to work, you would have to include the cost of maintaining your car and repairs. Public transport might be a cheaper option, also depending on which you choose. A way to cut transportation costs if you still want to drive yourself to work, would be to start a car pool.

- **Health care**—This is another big expense, especially if your employer doesn't offer health insurance. The price of your health care will vary based on the size of your family, your age, and what your health status is. People have been struggling to keep up with health care fees, because of the constant increases, and often don't have many options available. The accessibility and quality of the health care services in developing countries are severely affected by spikes in healthcare costs.

- **Food**—Not only the price of food but also how close you stay to a grocery store affects the cost of groceries in your area. Food prices increase almost everywhere, but they're often heavily dependent on the size of the store and how easily the store has access to goods. Stores that are smaller might have higher prices compared to supermarkets, because of extra fees owners have to pay for delivery of goods.

These are some of the main factors that influence a place's cost-of-living, but it's not limited to only this. Mixed and random costs like clothing, taxes, and other household expenses also play an important role.

Generally, the overall cost-of-living is also affected by the area's average income. Places with people who earn more money usually have a higher cost-of-living. Also, you have to consider the community's social habits, lifestyle, and access to resources into consideration.

Having a proper understanding of how cost-of-living works and how it affects you, makes it easier to create your budget and be more careful with your spending.

Comparing the Cost-Of-Living in Different Locations

Since the cost-of-living is monitored and regulated, an index has been created to help people see what it might cost to live there. Life in the city certainly costs more when compared to other suburban areas.

The index uses data that represents what an average way of life would be and how much of your yearly income will need to go towards it. This is done in all regions and is available to the public so they can see whether they can afford to live in a specific area. You can use it before moving to a different location or deciding on retirement areas, especially if you'd like to move abroad.

Different Cost-Of-Living Indexes

Social Security Administration's COLA

This is a yearly **alteration** made to the index for people living on Social Security benefits, called a Cost-Of-Living-Adjustment. As inflation affects prices of goods and services, an adjustment is made as a means of assistance.

Accra Cost-Of-Living-Index (COLI)

The Council for Community and Economic Research, is responsible for gathering and producing their collected data quarterly. This index is created by calculating how much residents spend on transport, food, health care, and utilities.

Understanding the Impact of Inflation on the Cost-Of-Living

You already know what inflation is and the effect it has on the value of money, so needless to say, the cost-of-living can be significantly increased when inflation occurs.

Planning for Unexpected Expenses

Yes, this again. You might not understand how big of a deal it is to go through life unprepared for unexpected events, but I assure you, ask anyone who had to face a major life change without any contingency plans in place, it must have been extremely tough.

Of course, the entire plan can't be mapped out from start-to-finish, but you can have most of the stressful part of it out of the way. From the death of a loved one to a sudden disability, these unexpected life events can turn your life upside down, and the help of savings can relieve some of the pressure.

Unexpected events don't only apply to negative occurrences. There are positive unexpected events, like inheriting a large amount of money, that can happen too. And sometimes, this unexpected fortune can be overwhelming and lead to poorly thought-out decisions.

To help you remain calm in such times, ask yourself what your plans are for the money. Do you want to cover the education fees of someone close to you? Is there someone you love that's in need of financial assistance? Or are there any charities you'd like to donate some money to?

What you're going to do with the money isn't the only thing to think about, you should also speak to a professional about any estate taxes that may come with the inheritance.

Chapter 7:
Banking

It is well enough that people of the nation do not understand our banking and monetary system, for if they did, I believe there would be a revolution before tomorrow morning. –Henry Ford

I'd like to cover some of the different kinds of accounts available and their uses. This isn't only important for your general account, but particularly important for people who have diverse financial portfolios, as it helps you understand which one is correct for the function you want it to have.

Let's get straight to it.

- **Savings**—The best part of a savings account is that it can be easily linked to your check account. The funds are taken from your check account on a set date, and placed into the savings account with ease. Since many people prefer separating their spending money from their savings to avoid the risk of using it accidently.

- **Checking**—This account is the most commonly used account, as it helps you control your income and expenses. It offers an organized list of every expense you pay from it and every penny paid into it. This makes the outline of your financial activities much clearer. You can withdraw your money from an ATM without waiting periods or heavy fees.

- **Certificate of deposit (CD)**—These are used to store your money temporarily, usually for a specific timeframe. The shortest timeframe would be six months and the longest, five years. That said, you can earn returns on these accounts and the longer you leave your money in there, the bigger returns you'll get. It's how you'll receive the key benefits of having such an account too. Leaving the money in your account for the full period agreed on is recommended, because early withdrawal leads to penalties.

Online Banking, Mobile Banking, and ATM Services

Online Banks

This is not the same as banks with online accessibility. These are banks that have no physical facility for you to go to in person, their operations are done strictly online. Because they don't have to worry about office space, equipment, and operations, they save a good amount of money. This allows them to share that with their customers by offering above average interest rates and reduced monthly fees.

ATM

It stands for *automated teller machine* and offers the standard transactions without the need for bank workers' help. It's basically an electronic machine where you put your bank card into and enter your pin. You can then choose the basic functions you'd like to use. The functions are quite limited and people mainly use it to pay money to someone else or withdraw their cash.

Mobile Banking

Mobile banking is exactly that, banking from your mobile. In other words, most of what you can do at a bank is at your fingertips, since you can literally be on the road and pay bills or transfer funds around. There are tons of mobile banking apps that are simple and easy to understand.

Online Banking

This type of banking is when a bank has their facilities available online too, not only at ATMs or on apps, but your computer too. Online banks usually have the most functions available out of three options, because some apps, while still offering more than ATMs, still have a limit to what actions can be performed via cellphone.

The perks when it comes to online and mobile banking, is that it can be done from anywhere and at any time of the day.

Overdraft Protection, Loans, and Mortgages

I know these terms are a bit much and will be hard to remember, but the point here is to get you familiar with them. You can always come back to the book to double check for help if you find yourself forgetting some of the things you're learning.

Overdraft protection is just a type of service offered with some accounts to help cover costs of some transactions.

You should already have a good idea what a loan is. This is something you get from a financial institution where they give you a certain amount of money up front, and you agree to pay them a certain amount back for a number of months or years. The amount you are given is referred to as the principal amount and which will be less than the total repaid.

A mortgage is also a sort of loan but the repayment is secured to an asset like a property.

Setting up a Savings or Checking Account

You're bound to open these once you're ready to take your finances to the next level, and I want to make sure you know what the process involves and what to look out for. As explained before, a checking account is used to receive deposits into, as well as make payments from. And a savings account is used to store money that will not be used immediately, so that money can earn interest.

But how do you know which of the many types of savings and checking accounts are the best choice? Simple, you compare the features of the different accounts and choose the one with the most reasonable and beneficial ones.

Here are some major things to look for

- How convenient is it to get to the ATM or bank when you need assistance?

- Are there minimum balance requirements and who offers the lowest?

- Do they have online or mobile banking available?

- Is there any insurance coverage?

- How much interest can be earned annually?

- Which one's monthly fees are most affordable?

- Is the company verified?

It's essential that you keep these questions in mind as you shop for service providers because the sales consultants at every institution will have a whole list of why their product is best, but only you can decide if that really is the case. And the only way to do that is to know which questions to ask.

Once you know which account you want and who you're going with, make sure you have all the necessary documents they will need for your application.

These documents are

- social security number

- contact details

- proof of address

- identification cards, like a passport etc.

- date of birth

Every place is different, and while the above is the usual required documents you can expect them to ask, some places might ask for more information depending on the situation. Don't worry about the safety of your personal information because these organizations are legally bound by data protection acts and treat sensitive info with the utmost caution.

Keep Track of Transactions and Manage Account Information Securely

You have seen how simple digital banking makes life and since this is the option most people choose nowadays; I want to stress the importance of protecting your data again. Yes, you're working through an app or online site, but if you don't have the software to protect your information, you risk losing all your money. Don't click on unknown sites, even when you're just browsing social media. You'd be surprised to learn how quickly unsecure links can access your info, even if you clicked out of it as soon as you saw.

Make sure you go over your transactions statements often and know what each transaction was for, because not doing this might lead you to overlook activities that you didn't authorize.

You can find out if there's anything more you can do to protect your accounts from your credit unions or directly with your bank.

Contact your bank as soon as you see activity you don't recognize.

Set Up Alerts That Help Monitor Account Activity

This is a function that is available with nearly all banks and financial institutions, because people all want to be kept in the loop 24/7. Automatic notifications are sent to your emails or phone when any money is withdrawn, deposited, etc. Even though you're going to be keeping an eye on the account yourself, it's extra peace of mind knowing you will get a notification about everything, in case you forget.

Online Security Measures

There are ways to lower your chances of putting your data at risk and they include the following.

- **No public Wi-Fi**—It might seem like a blessing in disguise when you're out-and-about and come across an open Wi-Fi connection, but the risks are not worth the reward. Public connections have very little security and are the easiest ways to hack into people's systems. Rather connect only to secure networks.

- **Update your own software security**—Anti-malware and anti-viruses are extra costs but it's better to pay that little extra now, than wait to be hacked and have your accounts cleaned out. Don't delay or ignore system updates. Each time it **prompts** you to update the software, run the update! It's being suggested for a reason. The system may have found weaknesses in its software and improved it, but it's up to you to run it so you can be protected.

- **Official sites only**—I've told you all about the https you need to look for, so be sure to remember this. Don't go to sites through links that were sent to you by email, as this is one of the most common ways to unknowingly land on an unsecure site.

- **Two-step authentication**—Also mentioned previously, two-step authentication is used simply to add another level of protection. So, even if a hacker has your online banking information, they will have a harder time getting past this authentication because you are sent new codes each time or have to log in using **biometrics**—You can ask your bank for help setting up this function.

Interest and Fees Associated With Banking Products

As great as banks are with storing your money and making it worth it, there are many fees people don't prepare for when opening accounts, and this often shocks them when they review their monthly statements. Do yourself a favor and find out about what fees to expect now, rather than seeing it be taken from your account first.

Interest is anything but new to you at this point, and you now know that it is accumulated monthly, quarterly, or annually. Does it confuse you why the bank would add money on top of the money you're just leaving in an account?

You're not alone, the idea of interest can be a bit difficult to wrap your head around, so let me shed some light.

People who have accounts with savings and leave them untouched, are given the gift of earning extra money (interest) on those funds, because the bank takes their saved money and lends it out. Don't stress, this is also why loans have interest fees charged on them, because the interest borrower has to pay is used to balance out the interest you need to get for not touching your money. So, it's a cycle that runs continuously; rewarding those who don't spend their money and taking more from those who do.

What Is Simple and Compound Interest?

I briefly went over what these two terms meant but I want to make sure you properly understand what each type of interest entails, so let's recap for a minute.

Simple interest refers to a strict interest rate added to the money someone borrows from a bank or finance company. This is the interest you pay for getting to use someone else's money.

Compound interest, on the other hand, is what you get paid for leaving your money in the account for the bank to use. When I explained it earlier in the book, you saw that compound interest is interest that earns more interest, which is the reason why this kind of interest is the most desirable.

What Do Bank Fees Entail?

Bank fees are any fees charged by a finance company for the maintenance of accounts, setting up of accounts, operational costs, transfer fees, transaction fees and more. They are basically fees you have to pay for using the bank's services and even though they might not be much on their own, these fees can be quite hefty when added together.

Typically, bank fees are charged for:

- **ATM services**—This is not a monthly fee and is charged when you use the service. It's not only because you're using the ATM that you're getting charged, but of course, the ATMs need servicing, money needs to be placed into it regularly, and the banks have to ensure that ATMS are fully functional, so there's a charge to enjoy this service.

- **Late payments**—Missing the date you were supposed to transfer money into your account comes at the cost of paying late fees. The banks penalize you for not being responsible and wasting resources used on your account for collections or failed transactions.

- **Minimum account balance**—Not all banks have this fee but there are those who do, so before you let your account go below the minimum balance allowed, find out what that balance is and how you can keep your account in line with it. Your account won't even have to be below the balance for a long time for you to be charged, as little as one day is enough for you to be slapped with this fee on your next statement.

- **Overdraft**—This is a fee charged when your account has less than zero in it. It means your account is in overdraft and you'll definitely have to pay this back. Sometimes there is even interest charged on this amount. It's because you now owe the bank, rather than the bank owing you.

- **Non-sufficient funds (NSF)**—You're charged this fee when a transaction is being made but your account doesn't have the full money to complete the transaction. Because the transaction was attempted and failed, the bank reverses the transaction and penalizes you for it.

- **Transfer and withdrawal**—Using the functions to withdraw and transfer money from your account is often free for a certain number of times a month. If you go over that number or draw from ATMs that don't belong to your bank, you are charged a fee. You can also be charged for a specific type of transfer, like wiring money to an ATM for someone else to withdraw.

Financial Planning and Decision-Making

Whether you're planning on investing, starting a business, or living life normally, financial planning is the only way to ensure you get where you need to be, with as little struggles as possible. Diversification is going to be one of your best friends if you plan to make the most out of your money and savings will be the driving force of your financial growth.

Financial planning makes decision-making easier because you have a clear mental picture of what you can afford and what you can't. You also know exactly where you are in the process of working toward your life goals, so you're less likely to risk throwing it away for short-term fun.

When you feel like it's too much work, keep watching videos of the house, car, clothes, or lifestyle you want. Use it as motivation to keep going because in the end, it'll be the best decision you could've made for yourself and your family.

Chapter 8:
Understanding Tax

You don't pay taxes-they take taxes. –Chris Rock

Tax or *taxation*, is enforced by the government of a country on its occupants. These fees are **obligatory** and refer to different kinds of taxes. There is no choice in whether you want to pay tax as it's against the law not to.

What Is Tax Collection?

Income tax withholding is the most prominent tax collected in the US annually. Earners and workers are both liable for paying taxes; however, since most workers prefer to pay their taxes off bit-by-bit with each salary over the course of the year, the tax collection in their case differs from earners. Many earners go with the option of paying it in one go. We file tax returns to check if we've paid more than we should have on taxes and if so; the IRS refunds that money.

Types of Taxes

Taxes are charged on various things. Below are the different kinds of taxes:

- **Corporate taxes**—This is the kind of taxes businesses pay and is deducted from the entire company's income. Corporate taxes usually have a fixed rate.

- **Income taxes**—Refers to the taxes deducted from all income earners in a country. Any form of income earned, so not only salary and wages but also returns on investments, tips, unemployment checks, etc. For people earning higher than a certain amount, tax on your social security benefits should be expected.

- **Payroll taxes**—This tax is deducted from your salary before even paid to you as your employer is responsible for this deduction and pays it to the government on your behalf. These taxes are for a range of things.

- **Tariffs**—This tax is relevant when a country imports goods and services from another. This is why you pay extra when you want to buy something from outside the US, as the government aims to encourage purchases within the country more.

- **Sales taxes**—This is what you pay on the items you buy or services you pay for. It's charged during the purchase and there can often be more than one single purchase. For **merchants**, however, this amount is not a problem because they buy from wholesalers and avoid this fee.

- **Property taxes**—This is a homeowner's tax and is determined based on the value of their property. Many places also charge a property tax on vehicles owned, and the funds go towards various services like the construction of roads or emergency response services.

- **Estate taxes**—You'll only be charged estate taxes if the property you own is worth more than a certain amount.

The amount you pay on your federal income tax depends on your income and whether you file your taxes as a single or married person. The more you earn, the higher the percentage of tax you can expect to pay.

The Role of Taxes

Taxes are crucial to the country's operations and generate the country's main income. It's used to supply, repair, preserve, and refine the public services we rely on.

These include: transport routes, welfare, educational facilities, and emergency services.

Since there are different kinds of taxes, who has to pay what depends on the type of tax. For instance, everyone pays sales taxes because it's added to goods and services, anyone earning an income will pay income taxes, and corporate taxes are only collected from business owners.

Although, how much (if at all) depends on the location and tax laws of that area.

Progressive and Regressive Tax

Progressive tax refers to tax rates that can be adjusted depending on the situation. For example, income tax is higher when you earn more. That said, it's possible to have the first few thousand dollars of your income free from income tax, and this is called an *exemption*.

Regressive tax refers to tax rates that are fixed. This type of tax often includes sales and property taxes. It means everyone pays the same amount of taxes here.

Importance of Paying Your Taxes

It's essential that you file your taxes early so you avoid any late penalties, as well as have a proper understanding of what you've paid in tax. As much as it's possible for you to have overpaid on taxes, you could also have underpaid and the owed money has to be paid back. Gathering this info early will count in your favor, because you'll still have time to set up an arrangement.

The only way to address any trouble you might be having with making payments is to contact the IRS and inform them. They'll be more than happy to provide you with alternative options.

Avoiding Taxes

The frequency of when tax is charged depends on the type of tax. As you know, sales taxes are paid immediately with the purchase, whereas income tax is charged monthly or annually. It also depends on the country as it may differ from one place to another.

Ignoring your tax-payer duties is an extremely big problem and can land you in major trouble.

You might get charged a penalty that requires one payment, or you could end up with one that requires you to make multiple payments. If you're not able to make the payments, one of the worst things that could happen is a charge being placed on your assets until. You can also be blocked from using certain services or goods, which is nothing compared to the possibility of the IRS seizing the property or assets you own, as a way to repay your debt. There's really nothing you can do when this happens, so do your best to adhere to your tax responsibilities.

Exemptions, Tax Brackets, and Tax Codes

You should already have an idea of what a tax exemption is. It's the privilege offered to people with certain circumstances to get out of paying taxes. For example, earning below a specific amount or running a non-profit organization.

A tax bracket is the category people are placed into which shows how much tax they pay, based on their income, among other things.

The main point here I'd like to cover is: the tax code.

The tax code refers to the official law that determines what a government expects business owners, married couples, and singles to pay on the various taxable services and goods. It is understandable that these funds are often met with complaints from the public; however, these fees are not going anywhere.

Tax codes of a country are the units responsible for setting up and arranging the various taxes residents will pay. In the US, we have the Internal Revenue Code (IRC), whereas other countries will have their own. For example, The UK has HM Revenue and Customs (HMRC), and Canada has the Canada Revenue Agency (CRA)(Scott, n.d.).

The Importance of Filing Taxes and Keeping Records

As you've seen throughout this book, keeping track of all your financial activities is highly encouraged, so monitoring and recording your tax activities are no different.

It's in your best interest to

- review financial statements
- monitor cash inflow and outflow
- compile your tax returns beforehand

- account for all items listed on your tax returns

- determine where all income is coming from

At the end of the day, keeping track of everything in such detail is never going to be something fun, unless accounting is your calling. Still, it's extremely necessary and mainly for your benefit. You might want to have paper and digital copies of all your recorded information, in case something happens to either one. Make sure the ones kept digitally are kept on secure devices and encrypted.

Chapter 9:
Career and Money

The future depends on what you do today. –Mahatma Gandhi

An employer is a business owner who hires people to work for them. They decide when, where, and how work will be performed and they're responsible for paying salaries, benefits, overtime, and more.

An employee, on the other hand, is the person who has been hired to perform a certain job for that company. The amount you earn depends on your type of employment, the type of job, your experience, and more. Employers will usually tell you what the requirements are to earn the amount they are willing to offer for that role, but in some cases, even if you don't meet all the requirements, they might still hire you and simply adjust the salary.

Income you earn doesn't only apply to the money you work for and can consist of other kinds of active income (benefit payouts like union strike benefits), or passive income (investment returns, etc.). *Earned income* is what they use to describe the income you get by working or performing a specific task for it, and *unearned income* is what they use to describe money given to you as a gift or returns on investments—Basically any money you didn't have to work for.

Earned income is always subjected to taxes, but unearned income has to meet specific standards before taxes are collected from it.

Different Types of Employment and Earning Income

There's no denying that working is important. Sure, we all have days when we feel like we can't go on, even in our youth, but working teaches us valuable life lessons. Also, it's great earning your own money so you don't have to rely on someone else to look after you.

That said, most people are working in places they never dreamed of working simply because it's the only way to pay the bills. This is the case for too many people and is often why many of them jump from job-to-job, or wake up feeling miserable about having to go back there.

The key to positive work experiences is, in part, your attitude towards your job and working in general, but mainly choosing the job that fits your personality and goals. It's the easiest way to ensure you stay motivated and work hard. There are different types of employment options to choose from and this chapter is designed to help make choosing your career easier.

Notice, I didn't say job. This is because there are fundamental differences between a job and a career.

The bulk of people only have jobs, which is just a position of employment at a company, whereas others are not only working in a specific position until the end of time, they're working tirelessly toward what the profession they are passionate about. Unlike a job, a career takes a long time to establish, often needing additional studies after high school, and training throughout your life.

People choose to do this so they can become masters of their **craft** and build a good **reputation** in their field. Careers offer more security than jobs sometimes. There have been countless times where people go to work and are handed a letter that says they shouldn't come back after whatever date because the company is closing down.

Still, even though having a career is better and should be your main goal, you're going to have to hold a few jobs before you get to that point.

Let's discuss the primary forms of employment you'll hear about., which are: full-time, part-time, contracting, and casual.

- **Full-time**—It's basically a permanent agreement between you and the employer. It's when the number of hours you have to work in a week is fixed and usually not lower than 38 hours. You have all kinds of benefits available to you, like paid time off work in the form of annual leave, sick leave, and if your company celebrates federal holidays, these too. Entering a full-time employment agreement makes leaving the company to work elsewhere tricky, because you have the legal duty to work out a certain amount of time first, called a notice period. The notice period is so that the company can use the time to get someone to replace you. Your notice period is longer when you've worked for the company for a longer time. The income related to full-time employment is received like **clockwork,** either weekly, fortnightly, or monthly.

- **Part-time**—The basic benefits and principles of full-time employment apply here too, except they depend on hours worked. For instance, even though you'll also get annual and sick leave, you'll have to work a certain number of hours before you're allowed that time off. The biggest difference between part-time and full-time is the number of hours you work weekly. Since 38 hours is the average for full-time workers, a part-time worker's hours tend to be less. Leaving the company might also not be as easy as one-two-three, meaning there might be a notice period to be worked here too.

- **Contracting**—Here, the game changes a bit since you are working for yourself and offer your services to people at your own rate. You are not viewed as an employee, so you don't get any of the benefits they do. Also, considering how you're basically self-employed, you will need to pay extra taxes (e.g., corporate taxes) and register yourself as a small business if you meet the criteria. Unlike part-time and full-time employees, your income isn't paid on a set date. You usually have to complete the job first, **invoice** your customer, and they'll make payment from there. With other types of employment, your employer deducts your taxes from your gross income and pays it to the government on your behalf, but in contract work, you are responsible for doing that yourself. There is no paid time off work here as you are only paid for hours worked.

- **Casual**—This another one where paid time off is not offered; however, you do have an employer. How many hours a week you work varies greatly from week-to-week and you will also only be paid for the hours you've worked. The rate you get hourly is normally higher than full or part-time workers', because you don't get the same benefits they do. You're also more likely to work on the days those workers are off, like weekends or federal holidays (if the company remains operational over those days).

These are the main kinds of employment and most arrangements in everyday work life. Although, there are less common employment types I'd like to share with you too.

They are

- Agency employment: This is when a company whose sole purpose is to find workers for another company, hires you for the job. You are employed by the agency but work for the company. You don't take any issues up with the company, but rather the agency who hired you. Because you're not a company employee, you won't always get the same benefits as them. Instead, your contract with the agency will list all the things you're **entitled** to. Don't panic, you are still protected by basic employment conditions and regulations, so it's not like you're a lamb to the slaughter. You still have to be treated fairly.

- Seasonal employment: This kind of employment is for a very brief period, often over summer or winter holidays. It's rare that your seasonal contract will be extended further than the agreed timeframe as companies tend to only hire seasonal workers for that time, because their part-time and full-time staff might have taken their annual leave or the company is just **understaffed** during those periods. Seasonal workers typically get paid the minimum hourly rate and can earn extra when working weekends. While they have a different set of rights, they can find out more by contacting the Workplace Relations Commission (WRC).

- Gig work: Similarly to contractors, gig workers don't work for an employer but for themselves. Whether you're seen as a small business depends on whether you meet the criteria in terms of income and operations. You also get paid for each gig only, and don't get benefits since you don't work for anyone. The hours you have to work depends on the gig itself.

- Young workers: Any child under 16 is forbidden from working. Of course, it depends on the type of work too. Starring in a film is not too problematic, but it's always best to check with the WRC first. Over 16s are allowed to do work that isn't too **straining** in order to get training and experience, but there are limits to how long and until what time they can work. They also consider your schooling responsibilities to ensure the work doesn't disrupt their education.

Understanding the Basics of Employment Laws

All workers have the right to a safe and healthy work environment, and in the US, The US Department of Labor is in charge of managing and implementing the laws that make this possible.

Workplace Health and Safety

The Occupational Safety and Health Administration (OSHA) governs health and safety conditions in the private sector. The majority of the public sector. Most of the public sector and self-employed don't fall under the OSHA. The role of the OSHA is not only to **enforce** these safety laws, but to also ensure people abide by them, because everyone has the right to work in an environment that's not dangerous.

They also have programs that make it possible for employees to report concerns without having to worry about losing their job or damaging their growth in the company as a result of it.

Some Main Employee Rights

A safe and healthy work environment is one of the most basic rights each employee has. It forms part of some of the most important rights every employee is entitled to, along with the right to not be harassed. This isn't all though, however, many employees will agree that not being discriminated against or harassed is very important in your workplace, as well as being able to join or found a union.

Unions are groups that aim to protect the rights of employees when they're not being fulfilled and negotiate for improvements. You do have the option of discussing this directly with your employee and one usually only involves the union when you're getting nowhere with your employer.

That said, below is a better list of the primary rights you should be aware of.

- **Discrimination free**—This is your right to work in a place without being harassed or treated differently because of things like being gay, a foreigner, a person of color, older, or any other reason. You can report any violation of your rights and will be advised on the next steps.

- **Family and medical leave**—Life happens to all and you have the right to take time off work to attend to such emergencies. The process might vary from company-to-company and may depend on your type of employment, but this is still one of your basic rights and cannot be overlooked.

- **Voting**—Every citizen has the right to vote, so don't be afraid to ask for time off work to fulfill this civil duty.

- **Health and Safety**—This, as you've seen, refers to the work environment. It doesn't only refer to safety equipment being readily available and no physical dangers, but also a mentally stimulating space. Verbal abuse in the workplace is unacceptable; however, there are occasions where some people are subject to it and should be reported immediately.

- **Privacy**—You have the right to privacy, meaning your employer has no authority to ask about your personal, non-work-related affairs. If it doesn't affect or go against your employment **mandates**, there is no need for them to know. Your employer also can't share your personal information with anyone else, and can be reported if they do.

- **Fair pay**—There are various minimum wage laws meaning a company can't pay you less than a certain amount for a particular job being done for however many hours. Your services come at a price and you have the right to be paid what you deserve.

Entrepreneurship Opportunities

Even though there aren't many **entrepreneurs** around, these people form an important part of the country's economy. They are often over-regulated which is why many of them take their business abroad. These individuals can significantly improve the state of a country's economy by job creation, innovation, and flexibility.

Entrepreneurs don't only offer new jobs, whether short or long-term, they also encourage other businesses to improve. This is because businesses are always competing with one another so the more options consumers have, the harder businesses will have to work to convince consumers to go with their product instead. Entrepreneurs also change people's approach to goods, services, and technology in general; paving the way for better, more convenient resources.

However, with all good things there are some bad too. Like how the uncertainty of success in entrepreneurship causes most people to steer clear from taking the risk. One has a lot more to lose when trying to start your business, compared to if you just go work for someone who's already had their business for 20 years. Over-regulations cause many entrepreneurs to take their business elsewhere, which negatively impacts their own country's economy.

Multiple Sources of Income

As the heading suggests, this involves having income coming from multiple places. It's obviously good to have a job and earn money through work, but having multiple sources of income makes life so much easier. Anything can happen with your job and not having another source of income can have some really horrible ripple effects, like losing your car or house.

This is why people find other ways to generate income on top of what they already get.

Some of these include:

- getting a part-time job. This is only relevant if you already work full-time. You might need extra cash, so because of the flexible hours part-time work offers, it is a perfect option for many. An example of this would be part-time waitressing, garden work or whatever else.

- starting affiliate marketing. This is when you have a social media presence and buy certain products or services and give reviews on it to your followers. You recommend the items and get paid for it.

- getting dividend income. Here, I'm talking about partial returns received from stock investments. If the company you invested in has good returns, they sometimes share it with the shareholders (people who have invested in the company).

- starting a side-hustle. It doesn't have to be an official new business and simply be you going around offering a service for some extra money like doing people's hair or nails for cash, tutoring students in lower grades, or babysitting.

Chapter 10:
Financial Decision-Making

A formal education will make you a living; self-education will make you a fortune. –Jim Rohn

This chapter covers the financial decision-making process and provides advice on how to stop yourself from impulse-buying. Further, there will also be discussions on whether seeking professional advice is necessary.

Why Are Informed Financial Decisions So Important?

Money and spending habits can cause major chaos in families and beyond, especially if everyone bringing in an income is not on the same page. Even governments who spend money carelessly end up putting their country in debt and fail to give the people proper resources.

They also increase taxes and place the burden of restoring the country's economy on its taxpayers, and this can lead to riots and strikes from the public. Such **turmoil** has a huge impact on the country's stability and can lead investors to go elsewhere. For this reason, providing the youth and older generations with financial literacy helps prevent or reduce future financial **catastrophes**.

Financial literacy is an essential part of the decision-making process, as it helps prioritize the most important expenses in a household and country as a whole.

Needs vs Wants

A lot of the time financial struggles are not because someone doesn't earn enough to support themselves, but rather because they have a distorted idea of what needs to be bought, compared to what they want to buy. Which is why it's so important to map out your needs and wants, and plan from there. The only way to successfully do this is to be honest about what you need and what you want.

You might think something is a need but when you look closer, the brand or item in general is not needed.

Needs are things that you absolutely can't survive without, so have a look at what you list as a need and see if that is the case with every item on there. This is not to say something that is a want for one person, can't be a need for you, but only you know why you "need" it, so only you can **differentiate**.

For example, the internet can be a want to most and still be a need for someone who works from home. This is where being honest with yourself is the key to properly separate your expenses.

Avoiding Impulse Buying

If you haven't personally done this or seen someone else do it, it can be hard to understand how or why people impulse-buy. It could be anything from needing a stress release to just seeing something you really want in that moment that causes you to buy something impulsively, but regardless of the reason, this is damaging to your financial security.

Thankfully, there are some things you can do to help reduce the chances of impulse-buys, and they are:

- **Leave some of your cards at home**—When you're out-and-about and see something you'd like to buy, it's much easier to do it if you have every single credit card you own on you. Because chances are you're going to justify why this purchase is okay at that moment, and then regret it later on. Be sure to take only one, which will be the one you use to do all the things you have to for that day. You need to make sure what the balance is beforehand, so you can have an idea of the impact your impulse-buy would have on that balance.

- **Ignore shopping sites**—There is a function on your settings you can use to limit or reduce the amount of advertisements you receive from online stores, I suggest you use it wherever possible. We spend a lot of time online and the easier the access to us, the bigger the chances of caving to sales that pop-up out of nowhere.

- **Rather spend on someone close to you**—: This can be hard because you might be asking yourself, *What's the point? I wanted this item, so why spend that money on another person?* Well, hear me out: If you spend the money on buying yourself that thing you saw that wasn't part of your budget, you could end up with **buyer's remorse**. Buyer's remorse can be so bad for your mental health since you actually give yourself anxiety over the purchase you made. It's when you're filled with regret either because it cost too much, it wasn't needed, or it's thrown your budget off (or whatever other reason). Now, when you spend that money on someone close to you instead, you're less likely to feel that way. Their genuine **gratitude** and appreciation makes the purchase feel worth it and doesn't leave you with a heaviness on your heart for spending that money.

- **Save up for spoils**—This is where having savings for personal enjoyment comes in. You know that you're going to want to reward yourself now and then, I mean, who wants to work day in and day out without the pleasure of using their hard-earned money to treat themselves? Saving a small portion every month means you'll have a mini-fund to go to when it's got enough to cover the cost of a small shopping spree for things you want. It should help reduce random urges to buy things, because you know your **spontaneous** shopping spree is coming up soon.

- **Moments over merchandise**—What I mean here is that spending your money on moments rather than merchandise (goods) is another better use of your money. This is another way buyer's remorse can be avoided, because you're creating memories that are much more valuable than something that's going to sit in your room until you decide to use it. Doing this helps give you a new perspective of what's important and what isn't.

- **Don't shop to relieve stress**—: As mentioned at the beginning of this section, so many people fall victim to this. Life gets them down with whatever problems and miseries, and to make themselves feel better, they go on a heat-of-the-moment shopping spree. This is meant to act as therapy and bring them back to a calm state of mind, but when they're feeling less stress and look back at their purchases, they might find more reason to be overwhelmed. It's a brutal cycle. If your head is all over the place and you don't know how to release that stress, spend some time in nature, go for a run, or do some breathing exercises. Allowing yourself to be controlled by emotion is never a good idea when it comes to your finances.

- **Check for charities**—This is also done to help put things into perspective for you. If you already have five pairs of shoes and see another pair you want, checking charities for people who lack basic things like food, water, health care, or education, will help **influence** you to make a smart decision. You can rather donate to one of these charities and feel proud of how you spent that money.

- **Observe how impulse-buys make you feel**— I've been talking about buyer's remorse quite a bit, but this isn't necessarily going to happen with every purchase or impulse-buy. When you do happen to buy impulsively though, be honest with how you feel about it afterwards. It doesn't have to be immediately after, maybe a few days later or even a few weeks later. Just be sure you're being one hundred percent honest about how buying that item made you feel in the beginning compared to how you feel later on. A lot of the time, it's regret. If that is the case, the next time you have the urge to do the same thing, take a moment to remember the last time you did and how you felt. It should surely help in the decision-making.

- **Create a purchase queue**—This will be similar to when you add items to your wish list on a shopping site, because you mark all the items you'd like to buy and can always go back when you have the money to buy those items before buying anything else. This is an extremely helpful way to ease your mind too, because you're not bothered by the fact that you didn't buy it, since it's on your purchase queue. Sometimes, by the time you have the money to buy the item, you've lost interest in it altogether and end up saving yourself from an unnecessary buy.

- **Research the product before buying**—Make it a rule if you help you stick to it. I can't tell you how many times you buy something, go to use it, and find it doesn't work the way it should or do what it's supposed to. Then, when you search for reviews on it, you find countless complaints and issues with it. This can become so frustrating, because it's an outright waste of money. Buying something is a huge commitment, especially with bigger buys, so it helps to check for reviews and do research before spending the money you worked so hard for on it. Even though there are many stores that offer returns and exchanges, you often have to battle to get them to understand why you no longer want the item, and whether you get your money back depends on the store's policy.

- **Make a shopping list**—It's up to you to stick to this list, but making the list to begin with is the first step. Write down or type in a notepad on your phone, every single thing you need to buy and don't buy anything else. Don't go into stores you don't have to while you're doing your shopping either, because you're only opening the door for temptation.

- **Treat yourself with free things**—Just because you should spoil yourself doesn't mean it always has to cost you. There are plenty of things to do that will be great for your **morale**, that doesn't involve spending loads of money. Depending on where you live, do some research on activities and events that you might be interested in that are free and use those as your reward to yourself when you've made financially smart choices.

- **Keep your eye on the prize**—This is always going to be one of the main things you can use to slap some sense into yourself when you feel like wasting. If you have pictures or videos of what you're working towards, have a look at them when the impulse hits you. Remind yourself why you're even doing this whole budget-thing in the first place and I'm sure you will be convinced to be patient. Achieving your goals will be much more rewarding that a pair of new headphones you didn't even need.

Impulse buys come in different forms and while you may be able to tell yourself it wasn't, the truth is, if it wasn't in your plan to buy it and something motivated you to buy it at that moment, then yep, it was an impulse buy. Therefore, you shouldn't make shopping decisions when your emotions are all over the place, nor should you cave in to buying things that are not on your list. This level of self-control will be one of the keys to positive spending habits and financial security.

Seeking Financial Guidance

This isn't only for people who don't have a clue where to begin when it comes to savings, financial plans, budgeting, etc. It's also for people who just want to get a second opinion on their own strategy and are open to suggestions to make things easier. Until you've actually shopped around for various financial products and services, you don't know just how much is actually out there and how overwhelming it can be. There's no shame in asking a professional for help and it will only benefit you in the end.

These people are trained to assist with things like investments and saving, retirement plans, buying your first home, using big sums of money wisely, and even how to handle unexpected events. You're not seeking help because you don't know what to do with that money, you're seeking help because you want to find out if that is the best way to use that money. Chances are the financial advisor can point you in directions you would never have thought of.

Be mindful of what you want though. Do you want guidance or do you want advice?

What's the difference you ask?

The difference is financial guidance is when you're giving a breakdown of the different options out there and is a very general overview of it all, whereas financial advice is specific to your situation. You will explain what you have and what your goals are, and then receive the financial advice on how best to achieve that.

You can either contact a restricted advisor or an independent financial advisor. The difference between the two is that restricted advisers often focus on one area only, like retirement; however, independent financial advisors have knowledge on various options. Make sure the financial adviser you speak to is registered, as there are plenty of phonies around. There's no reason to be scared of asking for proof that they are qualified to be handling your matter.

Conclusion

There is no passion to be found playing small—in settling for a life that is less than the one you are capable of living. –Nelson Mandela

Wow, we've reached the end of our journey and what a ride it's been!

I hope I've been able to shed some light on the financial world and change the way you see your allowance and any other monetary gifts. You can now say you have an above average understanding of how the financial scene works and what is necessary to be financially successful. Still, I'd like to recap some of the main points of the book, in case they've already slipped your mind.

If there's anything else you happen to forget as you go and put these new skills into practice, don't hesitate to come back for a quick refresher.

Value of Money and Time

It's already a good thing if you're putting money into a piggy-bank at home, but remember, that inflation and the time value of money means that the same amount of money now might be worth so much less in the future. This can be combated by the interest of savings accounts.

Savings accounts are the best friends the money you don't use immediately could possibly have, because it grows just by being kept in the bank.

Compound Interest

Let's not forget the wonderful gift of compound interest. This is when the interest you earn on your savings earns even more interest. It's like getting free money. Of course, it's not free money because the banks understand that it's really hard for most people to put money aside and leave it there, so they reward you for your sacrifice with this little gem. Compound interest is how people build wealth, which should be your primary goal. Working just to survive from one month to the next is no way to live, and if you want to experience true freedom and happiness, building wealth is the most important tool that'll help you get there.

Technology and Convenience

The world is changing, and nearly everything is going digital. Don't allow this to overwhelm you or cause you to make poor decisions because you don't know how best to use technology to help manage your finances. Ask someone for help with which apps are best to assist in financial planning and budgeting, because the convenience of these apps will make a noticeable difference in how you view this difficult task.

Diversification

This is a biggie. Remember how good debt works? It can open so many doors for a better life and long-term wealth, so be sure to keep your financial portfolio as diverse as possible. Of course, you still have to be careful with the types of credit you have on your credit history and ensure you are paying all of them in full and on time, as your credit score can either make or break you. Diversification is what is going to make banks and financial companies want to loan you money, so that you can grow your money and in return, grow their money.

Cash Flow

Keep your eye on your cash flow. This isn't just about making sure you keep track of how your money is coming in and going out, it's also about checking whether your cash inflow is constantly more than your cash outflow. Monitoring this regularly helps you see whether you might have to cut out or reduce some expenses to limit your cash outflow even more. Getting a good amount of money coming in is great on your record, but not if you're losing more than half of it within the first few weeks of every month.

Cost-Of-Living

The cost-of-living is always going to be a major factor in where you live and where you should aim to live. As you've seen, big cities tend to have higher costs of living because of the higher demand and accessibility to resources, higher earning potential, and number of occupants. If your goal is to one day live in the big city, do the necessary research to see approximately how much it'll cost you to live there comfortably and work towards. You might have to adjust your budget here-and-there, but it'll be worth it.

Taxes

Taxes will follow you until the end of time so make peace with it now and strategize how to best manage your taxes. You don't want the IRS knocking on your door to seize your assets because you were too lazy to file your tax returns. Filing your returns doesn't have to be too much of a task as you can always minimize how much you have to do by regularly reviewing your statements, gathering your documents well beforehand, making sure everything listed is accounted for, and specify exactly where all your income is coming from. Failing to file or pay taxes has serious repercussions like fines and confiscation of goods.

Don't let it get that far.

Employment

This is the gateway to setting yourself up for the life you've always wanted. It's important that you keep in mind that income doesn't only have to come from your employment.

Yes, it will make up the majority for the bulk of your income, especially at first, but your aim should be to use employment as a way to build your wealth to such an extent that you no longer have to work that boring job until you're 60-years-old. If you work wisely with your money in your youth, you could be one of those people chilling in restaurants at 11:00 am, with no care in the world. Or visiting the Caribbean for a month just because you had a good year and can afford it.

Most importantly though, use your youth to ensure that you can retire early. No-one enjoys having to strain themselves until their senior years. Working at a job 40+ plus and have still never been able to travel abroad or do something extraordinary.

Life was made for living, and financial literacy is going to make that possible!

Glossary

Accomplish: To complete or fulfill something through actively trying.

Accountability: The responsibility of your actions or being held responsible.

Accumulating: Collecting, or growing in number or size.

Advisable: Most recommended or logical.

Affordability: Being able to afford something.

Agricultural: Referring to anything related to natural land and the improvement of it.

Aimlessly: Relating to no direction or function.

Algorithms: System that uses step-by-step calculations for problem-solving or improvement, usually on technological devices.

Alteration: Making a change or adjustment to something.

Annually: Refers to something that takes place every year.

Antiques: Something that has higher value in its current time as a result of being from an older time.

Assessment: Using collected data to determine a particular result or form an opinion on something.

Assigned: To have given someone an assignment or project.

Average: Most common result or half-way between all possibilities.

Bankrupt: To have no financial valuables left, often confirmed by law.

Biometrics: Program that uses biological features of people to identify them. Often used in digital security.

Brokerage account: An account specifically for investments as it allows the purchase of different investments.

Catastrophes: Occurrences that cause severe damage and chaos.

Category: A placement of groups of things that share similar traits.

Clockwork: Slam term used to describe when something happens as expected each time.

Colognes: A liquid that has been mixed with aromatic oils.

Contrast: Used when things being compared are very unalike.

Contributions: A portion given to a bigger part of something.

Complex: Refers to being made up of many difficult to understand parts.

Counterproductive: Working against the decided goal.

Craft: Refers to a skill that has been perfected through ongoing improvements.

Credible: Having supporting evidence to be believed.

Crippling: Something that makes one unable to move or function.

Criteria: A list of traits to be met to meet a certain standard.

Crucial: Extremely important.

Currency: Refers to a form of money, decided on from country-to-country.

Deductions: Refers to the reduction or lessening something.

Definitions: An explanation of what something means.

Devastating: When something causes extreme shock or damage

Differentiate: To understand what makes things different from each other.

Distribute: To stretch or expand across various sections.

Enabler: Someone or something that promotes a particular result.

Encourage: To provide support or persuasion.

Encrypted: Something that has been set up in a way that details are hidden.

Enlist: To select the use of someone or something for assistance.

Entitled: Refers to the right to specific rewards and advantages.

Entrepreneurs: Individuals who risk starting a business of their own.

Estimated: Something that has been roughly or somewhat measured.

Extraordinary: Uncommon, unique, outside of what is normally expected.

Extravagant: Unnecessarily above reasonable.

Exchange: Refers to giving something with the expectation of getting something else in return.

Evidently: Refers to something being clearly understandable or easy to be understood.

Familiarize: To get comfortable with something, to know something better.

Fluctuate: To move in unexpected directions; increasing and decreasing constantly.

Foster: To boost or promote improvements of someone or something.

Fortnightly: Occuring every two weeks.

Fundamentals: Refers to the basics or most important aspects something is based on.

Gratification: Refers to feelings of pleasure and satisfaction.

Gratitude: Feelings of being grateful for and appreciative of something.

Hedging: Refers to the act of defending or protecting something.

Imperative: Another way to say very important; cannot be ignored.

Implementing: Refers to putting something into practice.

Impulse: An unexpected and unplanned feeling to do something.

Incurring: To bring something about because of one's actions or choices.

Independence: Being able to do things for yourself without needing the help of others.

Inescapable: Referring to being unable to get around or away from something.

Influence: The power to affect or cause someone or something to behave in a desired way.

Inheritance: Refers to something that is passed down to another, usually by family.

Initial: Refers to the start or beginning of something.

Initiatives: Actions taken to promote a certain idea or cause.

Invoice: The bill for goods or services provided, breakdown of what each penny is being paid towards.

Insight: Possessing an in-depth understanding of something.

Jargon: Unique words and terms used only in certain jobs or divisions of something.

Journaling: The act of recording certain events, experiences, and occurrences on paper or digitally.

Landlord: Someone who owns a property allows others to live in it at a specific price.

Limited: Refers to something being able to go only as far as a certain point.

Mandates: An instruction or command that was given by an authority figure.

Mandatory: Refers to something being compulsory; having no choice in the matter.

Maximize: To use something to its full potential.

Merchants: Individuals who trade goods and services.

Milestone: An important point to reach that marks growth and improvement.

Mindful: To keep something in mind; remain aware.

Minimum: Refers to the lowest or least of something.

Morale: Refers to the mental and emotional attitude towards something.

Monopolize: To have the most control over operations.

Obligatory: Cannot be negotiated; mandatory.

Pandemics: An occurrence of a devastation that affects an entire country or the entire world.

Pawn Shops: Stores who lend money to customers in exchange for holding onto their goods.

Preserving: Making something last longer.

Prioritize: To assign the most importance to something or someone.

Principle: Standard beliefs of a person or many people.

Prompts: Suggests or recommends.

Provision: Refers to contributing something towards something else.

Quarterly: Every three months.

Ratio: A calculation or measurement that shows how amounts relate to each other in a certain situation.

Reckless: Refers to something that causes danger or harm unnecessarily.

Recurring: Occurring over and over again.

Refunded: To have your money for a purchase given back to you.

Reputation: A history of things people have shared and know about you.

Requirements: A set of needed traits to qualify for something or meet a certain standard.

Sacrifice: Giving up something for a greater reward.

Seasoned: Having more than enough experience with something.

Significant: Relevant to a great degree; important.

Short-sales: Selling stocks you only have a share in but don't own.

Spontaneous: Unexpectedly.

Strategy: A well throughout plan to do something.

Turmoil: A moment of chaos or disruption.

Unauthorized: Refers to something done that is not allowed.

Unavoidable: Cannot be avoided.

Understaffed: Refers to when there is not enough staff to manage a workload.

Unnecessary: Not needed.

Withdrawing: To remove something from something else.

Vast: Very broad or without end.

Visualize: To imagine or picture.

Vital: Important to the existence of something.

Vulnerabilities: Weakness of things that cause you to be weak.

References

A little debt is good for you. (2022, March 23). Optimate Financial Solutions. https://ofs.co.za/a-little-debt-is-good-for-you/

Active vs. passive investing: What's the difference? (n.d.). Investopedia. https://www.investopedia.com/news/active-vs-passive-investing/

Amadeo, K. (n.d.). *Cost of living: How to calculate, compare, and rank.* The Balance. https://www.thebalancemoney.com/cost-of-living-define-calculate-compare-rank-3305737

Baker, B. (2022, July 26). *6 tips for diversifying your investment portfolio.* Bankrate. https://www.bankrate.com/investing/tips-for-diversifying-your-portfolio/#six-strategies

Banking 101. (2022, November 2). Capital One. https://www.capitalone.com/bank/money-management/banking-basics/banking-products-and-services/

Banton, C. (n.d.). *Cost of living: Definition, how to calculate, index, and example.* Investopedia.

https://www.investopedia.com/terms/c/cost-of-living.asp

Bell, A. (n.d.). *6 reasons why you need a budget.* Investopedia. https://www.investopedia.com/financial-edge/1109/6-reasons-why-you-need-a-budget.aspx

Benefits of investing. (2018, June 29). Columbia Threadneedle Investments. https://www.columbiathreadneedle.co.uk/uk-capital-and-income-investment-trust-plc/insights/benefits-of-investing/

Bennett, K. (2022a, April 6). *What's the difference between fixed and variable expenses?* Bankrate. https://www.bankrate.com/banking/fixed-expenses-vs-variable-expenses/#save

Bennett, K. (2022b, July 7). *How to open a savings account: 6 steps to take.* Bankrate. https://www.bankrate.com/banking/savings/how-to-open-a-savings-account/#how-to-open

Borwick, K. (n.d.). *How to set and reach your financial goals.* Annuity.org. https://www.annuity.org/personal-finance/financial-wellness/financial-goals/

Buchenau, Z. (n.d.). *Why is budgeting important? 10 key benefits.* Be the Budget. https://bethebudget.com/why-is-budgeting-important/

Budgeting and the most common cost-of-living expenses. (2020, February 4). Capital One. https://www.capitalone.com/learn-grow/money-management/common-cost-of-living-expenses/

Budgeting quotes. (n.d.). Goodreads. https://www.goodreads.com/quotes/tag/budgeting

Carther Heyford, S. (n.d.). *Understanding the time value of money.* Investopedia. https://www.investopedia.com/articles/03/082703.asp

Cash flow definition. (2022, October 9). Accounting Tools. https://www.accountingtools.com/articles/what-is-cash-flow.html

Cash inflow vs outflow: What's the difference? (2022, August 1). FreshBooks. https://www.freshbooks.com/hub/accounting/cash-inflow-vs-outflow?fb_dnt=1

CFI Team. (n.d.-a). *Financial literacy.* Corporate Finance Institute. https://corporatefinanceinstitute.com/resources/management/financial-literacy/#:~:text=Benefits%20of%20Financial%20Literacy&text=better%20financial%20decisions-

CFI Team. (n.d.-b). *Time value of money.* Corporate Finance Institute. https://corporatefinanceinstitute.com/resources/valuation/time-value-of-money/

Chalbaud, S. (2015, October 7). *4 ways mobile apps can improve your money management.* Business Journals. https://www.bizjournals.com/bizjournals/how-to/funding/2015/10/mobile-apps-can-improve-your-money-management.html

Chen, J. (n.d.). *A beginner's guide to asset classes.* Investopedia. https://www.investopedia.com/articles/basics/11/3-s-simple-investing.asp

Comunale, J. (n.d.). Money as a unit of account: Purpose of money. Study. https://study.com/academy/lesson/money-as-a-unit-of-account-definition-function-

example.html#:~:text=Money%20is%20an%20
example%20of

Cost of living quotes (17 quotes). (n.d.). Goodreads.
    https://www.goodreads.com/quotes/tag/cost-
    of-living

Creating a budget. (n.d.). Bank of America.
    https://bettermoneyhabits.bankofamerica.com
    /en/saving-budgeting/creating-a-budget

Credit score. (n.d.). Investopedia.
    https://www.investopedia.com/terms/c/credit
    _score.asp

Cruze, R. (2022, December 22). *How to set financial goals.*
    Ramsey Solutions.
    https://www.ramseysolutions.com/personal-
    growth/setting-financial-goals

Cryptocurrencies. (n.d.). Reserve Bank of Australia.
    https://www.rba.gov.au/education/resources/
    explainers/cryptocurrencies.html#:~:text=Cryp
    tocurrencies%20are%20digital%20tokens.

Cussen, M. P. (n.d.). *Credit cards vs. debit cards: What's the
    difference?* Investopedia.
    https://www.investopedia.com/articles/person

al-finance/050214/credit-vs-debit-cards-which-better.asp

Different types of employment. (n.d.). Imb. https://www.imb.com.au/themoneytree/earning-an-income/different-types-of-employment.html

Different types of workers. (n.d.). Citizens Information. https://www.citizensinformation.ie/en/employment/types_of_employment/types_of_employment.html#startcontent

Differentiating fixed and variable expenses. (2022). In Building Blocks Teacher Guide. https://files.consumerfinance.gov/f/documents/cfpb_building_block_activities_differentiating-fixed-variable-expenses_guide.pdf

Duczeminski, M. (2015, August 8). *10 effective ways to avoid impulse buying.* Life Hack. https://www.lifehack.org/284944/10-effective-ways-avoid-impulse-buying

8 simple ways to save money. (n.d.). Bank of America. https://bettermoneyhabits.bankofamerica.com/en/saving-budgeting/ways-to-save-money

11 ways to stick to your budget. (n.d.). Valley First. https://www.valleyfirst.com/simple-advice/money/ways-to-stick-to-your-budget

Enang, W. (2022, June 2). *10 forms of money.* Proguide. https://proguide.ng/forms-or-types-of-money/

Farrington, R. (n.d.). *5 benefits of investing.* The College Investor. https://thecollegeinvestor.com/16912/5-benefits-of-investing/#t-1654539132152

Federal income tax calculator-estimator for 2022-2023 taxes. (2023, January 30). Smart Asset. https://smartasset.com/taxes/income-taxes

Fernando, J. (n.d.-a). *Financial literacy.* Investopedia. https://www.investopedia.com/terms/f/financial-literacy.asp

Fernando, J. (n.d.-b). *Time value of money explained with formula and examples.* Investopedia. https://www.investopedia.com/terms/t/timevalueofmoney.asp#:~:text=The%20time%20value%20of%20money%20means%20that%20a%20sum%20of

Fiduciary money. (n.d.). CEOpedia. https://ceopedia.org/index.php/Fiduciary_money

Financial plans vs. budgets. (n.d.). Wells Fargo. https://www.wellsfargo.com/financial-education/basic-finances/build-the-future/short-long-term-planning/budget-vs-financial-plan/

5 steps to setting your yearly financial goals. (2022, October 18). Principal. https://www.principal.com/individuals/build-your-knowledge/5-steps-setting-your-yearly-financial-goals

Fontinelle, A. (n.d.). *Setting financial goals for your future.* Investopedia. https://www.investopedia.com/articles/personal-finance/100516/setting-financial-goals/

Fortney, C. (n.d.). *Types and forms money.* Study. https://study.com/academy/lesson/money-definitions-and-basic-functions.html

4 reasons you need to pay your bills on time. (2022, July 5). New Mexico Bank and Trust. https://www.nmb-t.com/stories/financial-strength/4-reasons-to-pay-bills-on-time#:~:text=Paying%20bills%20on%20time%20leads

Friedman, M., & Meltzer, A. H. (n.d.-a). *Credit and money.* Britannica.

https://www.britannica.com/topic/money/Ce
ntral-banking

Friedman, M., & Meltzer, A. H. (n.d.-b). *Money*.
Britannica.
https://www.britannica.com/topic/money/Ce
ntral-banking

Geier, B. (2023, January 7). *10 common types of investments
and how they work*. SmartAsset.
https://smartasset.com/investing/types-of-
investment

Getting financial advice. (n.d.). Citizens Advice.
https://www.citizensadvice.org.uk/debt-and-
money/getting-financial-advice/

Getting started. (n.d.).
https://files.consumerfinance.gov/f/document
s/cfpb_your-money-your-
goals_savings_plan_tool_2018-11_ADA.pdf

Gorton, D. (n.d.). *Taxes*. Investopedia.
https://www.investopedia.com/terms/t/taxes.a
sp

Green, A. (2018, October 25). *Advantages & disadvantages
of e-payment*. Bizfluent.
https://bizfluent.com/how-7507577-make-
receive-payments-debit-card.html

Gross vs net income: Key differences and how to calculate. (2022, June 10). MBO Partners. https://www.mbopartners.com/blog/contracts -finance/gross-income-vs-net-income-what-is- the- difference/#:~:text=Gross%20income%20and %20net%20income

Hayes, A. (n.d.-a). *Cash flow.* Investopedia. https://www.investopedia.com/terms/c/cashfl ow.asp

Hayes, A. (n.d.-b). *Debit definition: Meaning and its relationship to credit.* Investopedia. https://www.investopedia.com/terms/d/debit. asp#:~:text=Debits%20are%20the%20opposit e%20of

Hayes, A. (n.d.-c). *Risk/Reward ratio: What it is, how stock investors use it.* Investopedia. https://www.investopedia.com/terms/r/riskre wardratio.asp#:~:text=What%20Is%20the%20 Risk%2FReward

Hicks, C. (2023, February 7). *How inflation affects your cost of living.* Forbes Advisor. https://www.forbes.com/advisor/investing/inf lation-cost-of-

living/#:~:text=%E2%80%9CWhen%20inflati
on%20rises%2C%20so%20do

How is a cost of living index calculated? (n.d.). Investopedia.
https://www.investopedia.com/ask/answers/1
00214/how-cost-living-index-calculated.asp

How to keep your current account safe and secure? (n.d.). Hdfc
Bank.
https://www.hdfcbank.com/personal/resource
s/learning-centre/save/how-to-keep-current-
account-safe

How to prepare for unexpected financial events. (n.d.).
Ameriprise.
https://www.ameriprise.com/financial-goals-
priorities/family-estate/prepare-unexpected-
events

How to stick to a budget. (2023, February 13). Ramsey
Solutions.
https://www.ramseysolutions.com/budgeting/
steps-to-help-you-stick-to-your-budget

Huffman, M. (2022, September 28). *How to choose a savings
account.*   Alliant.
https://www.alliantcreditunion.org/money-
mentor/what-to-look-for-in-a-savings-account

Importance of financial education in making informed decision on spending. (n.d.). Research Gate; Research Gate. https://www.researchgate.net/publication

Importance of saving money. (n.d.). IDFC FIRST Bank. https://www.idfcfirstbank.com/finfirst-blogs/savings-account/importance-of-having-savings

Income – saving = expense should be your equation to achieve your crorepati dream. (2018, March 11). Moneycontrol. https://www.moneycontrol.com/news/business/markets/income-saving-expense-should-be-your-equation-to-achieve-your-crorepati-dream-2525323.html

Income and expenses. (n.d.). Saylordotorg. https://saylordotorg.github.io/text_personal-finance/s06-01-income-and-expenses.html

Investing quotes (481 quotes). (n.d.). Goodreads. https://www.goodreads.com/quotes/tag/investing

Kagan, J. (n.d.-a). *Automatic savings plan.* Investopedia. https://www.investopedia.com/terms/a/automatic_savings_plan.asp

Kagan, J. (n.d.-b). *Understanding earned income and the earned income tax credit.* Investopedia.

https://www.investopedia.com/terms/e/earne
dincome.asp

Kenton, W. (n.d.). *Bank fees definition and different types.*
Investopedia.
https://www.investopedia.com/terms/b/bank-
fees.asp

Kritikos, A. S. (n.d.). *Entrepreneurs and their impact on jobs
and economic growth.* IZA World of Labor, 8(1).
https://doi.org/10.15185/izawol.8

Lake, R. (n.d.-a). *Do you need a savings plan? And how do you
make   one?*   Investopedia.
https://www.investopedia.com/make-savings-
plan-5208028

Lake, R. (n.d.-b). *How to protect your online banking
information.*   Forbes   Advisor.
https://www.forbes.com/advisor/banking/ho
w-to-protect-your-online-banking-information/

Lake, R., & Foreman, D. (n.d.). *Fixed vs. variable expenses:
What's   the   difference?*   Forbes   Advisor.
https://www.forbes.com/advisor/banking/bud
geting-fixed-expenses-vs-variable-expenses/

Loan   vs   mortgage. (n.d.).   Diffen;   Diffen.
https://www.diffen.com/difference/Loan_vs_
Mortgage

Money quotes. (n.d.). Goodreads. https://www.goodreads.com/quotes/tag/money?page=1

Muller, C. (n.d.). *How credit works: Understand the credit history reporting system.* Money under 30. https://www.moneyunder30.com/how-credit-works

O'Neill, B. (2009, February). *The benefits of saving money.* Rutgers. https://njaes.rutgers.edu/sshw/message/message.php?p=Finance&m=122#:~:text=Saving%20provides%20a%20financial%20%E2%80%9Cbackstop

Opperman, M. (n.d.). *Basics of taxes.* Credit. https://credit.org/blog/basics-of-taxes/

Pant, P. (n.d.-a). *What is the difference between wants and needs?* The Balance. https://www.thebalancemoney.com/how-to-separate-wants-and-needs-453592

Pant, P. (n.d.-b). *What's the difference between fixed and variable expenses?* The Balance. https://www.thebalancemoney.com/what-s-the-difference-between-fixed-and-variable-expenses-453774

Parker, T. (2019). *Calculating risk and reward.* Investopedia. https://www.investopedia.com/articles/stocks/11/calculating-risk-reward.asp

Payroll definitions. (n.d.). Patriot. https://www.patriotsoftware.com/payroll/training/definition/earning-types/

Peterdy, K. (n.d.). *Credit.* Corporate Finance Institute. https://corporatefinanceinstitute.com/resources/commercial-lending/credit/#:~:text=Credit%20is%20created%20when%20one%20party%20provides%20resources%20to%20another

Picardo, E. (n.d.). *Investing explained: Types of investments and how to get started.* Investopedia. https://www.investopedia.com/terms/i/investing.asp#:~:text=There%20are%20many%20types%20of

Pritchard, J. (n.d.). *How to open a bank account and what you need to do it.* The Balance. https://www.thebalancemoney.com/how-can-i-easily-open-bank-accounts-315723

Progressive and regressive tax systems. (n.d.). The Texas Politics Project.

https://texaspolitics.utexas.edu/archive/html/
pec/features/0400_01/slide3.html

Quotes about cash flow (60 quotes). (n.d.). Quote Master.
https://www.quotemaster.org/cash+flow

Reed, E. (2020, February 19). *Short-term vs. long-term
investing: What's the difference?* TheStreet.
https://www.thestreet.com/investing/short-
term-investing-vs-long-term-investing

Rights under employment law. (n.d.). Lawyerinfos.
https://lawyerinfos.com/understanding-
employee-rights-under-employment-law/

Saving. (n.d.). *Practical Business Skills.*
https://www.practicalbusinessskills.com/gettin
g-started/financial-basics/saving

Saving Money Quotes. (n.d.). Goodreads.
https://www.goodreads.com/quotes/tag/savin
g-money

Scheithe, E. (2020, May 5). *Online and mobile banking tips
for beginners.* Consumer Financial Protection
Bureau.
https://www.consumerfinance.gov/about-
us/blog/online-mobile-banking-tips-beginners/

Schmidt, J. (n.d.). *Income vs revenue vs earnings.* Corporate Finance Institute. https://corporatefinanceinstitute.com/resources/accounting/income-vs-revenue-vs-earnings/

Scott, M. P. (n.d.). *What is the tax code? How the U.S. tax code works and sections.* Investopedia. https://www.investopedia.com/terms/t/tax-code.asp#:~:text=A%20tax%20code%20is%20a

Scott, SJ. (2017, October 26). *How to stop impulse buying: 9 tips to curb your spending.* Develop Good Habits. https://www.developgoodhabits.com/impulse-buying/

Smits, L. (2021, April 19). *How to protect yourself from online fraud.* IT Governance USA Blog. https://www.itgovernanceusa.com/blog/how-to-protect-yourself-from-online-fraud

Sokunbi, B. (n.d.). *The 3 main ways to create multiple sources of income.* Clever Girl Finance. https://www.clevergirlfinance.com/blog/create-multiple-sources-of-income/

Stormont, B. (n.d.). *How to maximize compound interest.* Wikihow. https://www.wikihow.life/Maximize-Compound-

Interest#:~:text=You%20can%20maximize%2
0your%20earning

Tardi, C. (n.d.). *Financial portfolio: What it is, and how to create and manage one.* Investopedia. https://www.investopedia.com/terms/p/portf olio.asp#:~:text=A%20portfolio%20is%20a%2 0collection

Taxation. (n.d.). Corporate Finance Institute. https://corporatefinanceinstitute.com/resource s/accounting/taxation/

Taxes quotes (232 quotes). (n.d.). Goodreads. https://www.goodreads.com/quotes/tag/taxes

Team The WisdomPost & Sophia. (n.d.). *What is the difference between wealth and money?* The Wisdom Post. https://www.thewisdompost.com/money/diffe rence-wealth-money-answered/1607

10 inspirational career quotes—Start your success story today. (n.d.). Golden Rule. https://www.goldenrule.co.za/10-inspirational-career-quotes-start-your-success-story-today/

Thangavelu, P. (n.d.). *How inflation affects your savings.* Investopedia. https://www.investopedia.com/articles/investi

ng/090715/how-inflation-affects-your-cash-
savings.asp

Top 20 employment law facts you need to know. (n.d.). Startup
Donut.
https://www.startupdonut.co.uk/employees/e
mployment-rights/top-20-employment-law-
facts-you-need-to-know

Types of money. (n.d.). Macro Economics.
https://sites.google.com/somaiya.edu/macro-
econimics/money/types-of-money

Understand your credit. (n.d.). Equifax.
https://www.equifax.com/personal/understan
ding-credit/

Understanding credit. (n.d.). UC Berkeley.
https://financialaid.berkeley.edu/financial-
literacy-and-resources-financial-literacy-and-
resources/understanding-credit/

Understanding positive cash flow: 3 types of cash flow. (2022,
August 9). Shopify.
https://www.shopify.com/blog/positive-cash-
flow

Weltman, B. (n.d.). *Tax documents you should always keep.*
Investopedia.
https://www.investopedia.com/articles/person

al-finance/060315/tax-documents-you-should-always-keep.asp

What is budgeting? What is a budget? (n.d.). My Money Coach. https://www.mymoneycoach.ca/budgeting/what-is-a-budget-planning-forecasting

White, A. (n.d.). *What is overdraft protection and how does it work?* CNBC. https://www.cnbc.com/select/what-is-overdraft-protection-and-how-does-it-work/

Whiteside, E. (n.d.). *What is the 50/20/30 budget rule?* Investopedia. https://www.investopedia.com/ask/answers/022916/what-502030-budget-rule.asp

Why diversification matters. (2015). Fidelity. https://www.fidelity.com/learning-center/investment-products/mutual-funds/diversification

Why should I keep records? (n.d.). IRS. https://www.irs.gov/businesses/small-businesses-self-employed/why-should-i-keep-records

Woerner, J. (n.d.). *Money as a store of value.* Study. https://study.com/learn/lesson/store-value-overview-examples.html#:~:text=Money%20has%20a%20store%20of

Workplace safety & health. (n.d.). U.S. Department of Labor. https://www.dol.gov/general/topic/safety-health

Zucchi, K. (n.d.). *Why financial literacy is so important.* Investopedia. https://www.investopedia.com/articles/investing/100615/why-financial-literacy-and-education-so-important.asp